Each volume of
TWENTIETH CENTURY INTERPRETATIONS
presents the best of modern commentary on a
great work of literature, and an original introduction
to that work by an outstanding authority.
Analyzing themes, style, genre,
structural elements, artistic influences,
and historical background, the essays define
the place of the work in its tradition
and make clear its significance for readers of today.

D1311398

154178

TWENTIETH CENTURY INTERPRETATIONS

OF

DEATH OF A SALESMAN

A Collection of Critical Essays
Edited by
HELENE WICKHAM KOON

812
M647d
Yk

A SPECTRUM BOOK

Prentice-Hall, Inc., Englewood Cliffs, N.J. 07632

Alverno College
Library Media Center
Milwaukee, Wisconsin

Library of Congress Cataloging in Publication Data

Main entry under title:

Twentieth century interpretations of Death of a Salesman.

"A Spectrum Book."
Bibliography: p.
1. Miller, Arthur, 1915–   . Death of a salesman—
Addresses, essays, lectures. I. Koon, Helene (date)
PS3525.I5156D4377   1983   812'.52   82-18518
ISBN 0-13-198135-8
ISBN 0-13-198127-7 (pbk.)

This book is available at a special discount when ordered in large quantities. Contact Prentice-Hall, Inc., General Publishing Division, Special Sales, Englewood Cliffs, N.J. 07632

© 1983 by Prentice-Hall, Inc., Englewood Cliffs, New Jersey 07632
All rights reserved. No part of this book may be reproduced in any form or by any means without permission in writing from the publisher.
A SPECTRUM BOOK. Printed in the United States of America.

10   9   8   7   6   5   4   3   2   1

ISBN 0-13-198135-8

ISBN 0-13-198127-7 {PBK.}

Woodcut illustration by Edgar Blakeney © 1982
Manufacturing buyer: Barbara Frick

Prentice-Hall International, Inc., *London*
Prentice-Hall of Australia Pty. Limited, *Sydney*
Prentice-Hall Canada Inc., *Toronto*
Prentice-Hall of India Private Limited, *New Dehli*
Prentice-Hall of Japan, Inc., *Tokyo*
Prentice-Hall of Southeast Asia Pte. Ltd., *Singapore*
Whitehall Books Limited, *Wellington, New Zealand*
Editora Prentice-Hall do Brasil Ltda., *Rio de Janeiro*

Excerpts from *Death of a Salesman* by Arthur Miller, Copyright 1949 by Arthur Miller. Copyright renewed 1977 by Arthur Miller. Reprinted by permission of Viking Penguin Inc., and International Creative Management, Inc.

Excerpts from the Introduction to *Arthur Miller's Collected Plays*. Copyright 1957 by Arthur Miller. Reprinted by permission of Viking Penguin Inc., and International Creative Management, Inc.

The quotation from *Escape from Freedom* by Erich Fromm is used by permission of Holt, Rinehart, and Winston.

Excerpts on pages 52–53 from "The Death of the Hired Man" from *The Poetry of Robert Frost* edited by Edward Connery Lathem. Copyright 1930, 1939, copyright 1969 by Holt, Rinehart, and Winston. Copyright 1958 by Robert Frost. Copyright 1967 by Lesley Frost Ballantine. Reprinted by permission of Holt, Rinehart, and Winston, Publishers, and Jonathan Cape Limited.

The excerpt from Theatre Chronicle, "Old Glamour, New Gloom," review of *Death of a Salesman* by Eleanor Clark is used by permission of *Partisan Review*. Copyright Partisan Review, Volume XVI, Number 6, June 1949.

Contents

Introduction

Helene Wickham Koon

Arthur Miller was born in Manhattan on October 17, 1915, the second son of an affluent, immigrant clothing manufacturer. Three years old when World War I ended, Miller grew up during the prosperity and frenzy of the twenties—a prosperity and frenzy that ceased abruptly with the stock market crash of 1929. During the Depression that followed, his father's business collapsed and the family moved to Brooklyn, where Miller graduated from high school at the age of sixteen. Although his academic achievements were not remarkable, his claim to have passed through the public school system "unscathed" may not be quite an accurate description of a young man who found the inspiration to become a writer through reading Dostoevsky's *The Brothers Karamazov*.

For two years after high school, Miller worked in an automobile parts warehouse before enrolling at the University of Michigan, Ann Arbor, as a journalism student. He was soon involved in drama and, during his sophomore year, won the Avery Hopwood Award for his first play, *Honors at Dawn*, written during the ten days of spring vacation. The achievement is most unusual in view of his limited experience in the theater: he had seen only one play and had read some Shakespeare; he was so innocent of theatrical technique that he had to ask a fellow student how long an act should be.

After graduating from the university, Miller gained valuable stage experience through his work for the Federal Theater Project; equally valuable to him as a writer was his nontheatrical experience during World War II, when he toured army camps interviewing American soldiers for the film, *The Story of GI Joe*. Both were reflected in his first Broadway play, *The Man Who Had All the Luck* (1944). It was not a commercial success, but it did win the Theatre Guild National Prize, and it foreshadowed the kind of serious theme that characterizes his work. His second Broadway play, *All My Sons* (1947), was commercially successful and won the New

York Drama Critics' Circle Award. Two years later, *Death of a Salesman* began its long run on Broadway, won the New York Drama Critics' Circle Award as well as the Pulitzer Prize, and established him firmly as one of the most important American playwrights.

Those with a political bias saw *Death of a Salesman* and, later, *The Crucible* (1953), as political statements antithetical to the establishment. During the McCarthy era, Miller was refused a passport to attend the opening of *The Crucible* in Brussels.[1] In 1956, he was called before the House Un-American Activities Committee, where he refused to name suspected communists and was consequently convicted of contempt of Congress. Although the conviction was unanimously reversed by the Supreme Court in 1958, it brought him a good deal of adverse publicity.

Over the years, as the national atmosphere changed and it became evident that Miller was more interested in the human condition than in political doctrine, his work has been received more objectively. He has not always been a popular success—neither *A Memory of Two Mondays* (1955) nor *A View from the Bridge* (1955) was so considered—but he has become recognized as one of the most thoughtful and perceptive commentators of our time.

He has not restricted himself to the stage; his plays have also been produced on film and on television, and he has written in other genres as well: *The Misfits* was first a short story (1957), then a film (1961), and later, a novel (1962). He has also written critical articles and adaptations: his version of Ibsen's *Enemy of the People* was produced in 1950, and his television version of Fanya Fenelon's *Playing for Time* won an Emmy in 1981.

While his basic themes invariably center on moral values, his subjects and treatment vary widely: *The Misfits* has a western setting and, like *The Price* (1968), is directly concerned with personal integrity; *After the Fall* (1964) probes the mind of the guilt-haunted Quentin through his consciously reconstructed memory, touching on Miller's own relations with his second wife, Marilyn Monroe; guilt and family relationships are also at the heart of *The Creation of the World and Other Business* (1972), where the Biblical element provides a completely different tone. Miller also examines questions that link in with his Jewish heritage: his first novel, *Focus*

[1]This occurred in 1954. Two years later, he was issued a passport for six months only. Later still, it was restored in full.

(1945), dealt with a gentile mistaken for a Jew; his play, *Incident at Vichy* (1964), and his teleplay, *Playing for Time*, treat the enormity of the holocaust in terms of the individual caught up in the torment.

Miller's work combines a deep concern for ordinary persons and their values with a strong sense of theater. As a child of the Depression who matured during the traumatic years of the Second World War, he takes a serious view of the world. He is concerned with large issues, with values, morality, and justice. He does not present these issues as abstract philosophical concepts, but in terms of individuals facing crises in what appear externally to be quite ordinary circumstances. His protagonists are distinctly non-heroic; unexceptional in quality of character, social position or power, they are not outstandingly good or evil, their lives do not affect a wide circle, and, if they fall, they do not take nations down with them. In the normal course of events, they might go un-noticed; yet each is confronted with the kind of situation that forces his or her best and worst qualities to the surface. More importantly, they are drawn with understanding, compassion, and a respect for human dignity that lifts them from the mundane and relates them to the profound questions of the contemporary world.

Critics have sometimes disagreed with the substance of Miller's plays, particularly in the late forties and early fifties when politics often colored reviewers' opinions, and Miller was considered a dangerous radical by those who saw his work as propaganda for left wing ideology. But however much they may have disliked the content or ideas, none of the critics charged him with ineffective theater. He has an intuitive sense of the dramatic moment, and his grasp of its power has been equaled by few. Utilizing the tech-niques and technology of the modern stage, he builds story, character, and tone simultaneously through scenes of memorable vitality and intense impact.

While all of Miller's work consistently demonstrates his concern for humanistic questions and his mastery of theatrical technique, *Death of a Salesman* is an especially noteworthy example. When it opened on February 10, 1949, it was hailed as an original and compelling insight into the American scene. It was called "one of the finest dramas in the whole range of the American theatre,"[2] and "not only by all odds the best play to have been written by an

[2]Brooks Atkinson, *New York Times*, February 11, 1949.

American this season, but a play which provides one of the modern theatre's most overpowering evenings."[3] Others saw it as "one of the most concentrated expressions of aggression and pity ever to be put on the stage,"[4] or as "a great American tragedy, shattering to the audience, overwhelming in its implications, cutting to the root of the poisonous fruits of the success rule of life."[5]

It was indeed shattering, and New York audiences were deeply moved by Willy Loman's fate. To some, he represented the failure of the American dream; to others he was the common man destroyed by progress; a few saw the play as a capitalistic/communist statement,[6] but whether the terms were personal, philosophical, or political, it was generally agreed that it reflected the mood of the times. It was, however, more than a topical success: *Death of a Salesman* speaks as clearly a generation after its inception as it did in 1949, and it has become a standard work in anthologies of twentieth-century drama.

Death of a Salesman is also a new kind of play, but it is not to deny Miller credit for originality to add that he has worked within tradition—several, in fact. More than any other single factor, perhaps, his eclecticism marks him as a writer of the twentieth century, for he has taken certain elements of the past and re-fashioned them into a single, unified, and original creation. Indeed, the fact that *Death of a Salesman* fits into several traditional theatrical categories (although into none absolutely) has caused much discussion among critics who have tried to measure it against a single yardstick.

The most frequent debate has centered on the question of tragedy. Most critics have agreed the play does not fall under the classic definition of tragedy as a serious action, complete in itself, evoking pity and terror in order to produce catharsis. Separate from this, but usually considered with it, is the question of the tragic hero—in Aristotelian terms, a great man of flawed good-

---

[3]John Mason Brown, "Seeing Things: Even as You and I," *Saturday Review of Literature*, 32 (February 26, 1949), 30.

[4]Daniel E. Schneider, *Theatre Arts* (October 1949), p. 20.

[5]Euphemia Van Rensselaer Wyatt, *Catholic World* (April 1949), p. 62.

[6]Eleanor Clark, in *The Partisan Review* Vol. XVI, no. 6 (June 1949), gave it a scathing review, commenting that the scene in which Willy is fired "comes straight from the party line literature of the 'thirties . . . ."

ness. Prior to the nineteenth century, "greatness," in the short-hand of the stage, was shown as social or political standing, but in the last 150 years, the emphasis has shifted to moral and humane qualities without much regard for position. A modern critics asks:

> Is such a human, humanly protested atrophy of the self not tragic? In the last analysis, your consent stands and falls together with your judgment of the world in which Willy Loman is lost and which can, if you choose it, display such remarkable semblance to your own world. . . . This choice of loss, was it his? Was it properly his own, if assumed under such massive pressure of the many others, could he stay one against the crowd and "to his own self be true?" That such a choice is possible and almost required in this world, may be for all who count themselves as living in it—tragic.[7]

Certain elements of classical tragedy are clearly present, if serious-ness of theme, structure, and inevitability are translated into modern idiom. In such terms, "the common man is as apt a subject for tragedy as kings were," said Miller, for "if the exaltation of tragic action were truly a property of the high-bred character alone, it is inconceivable that the mass of mankind should cherish tragedy above all other forms, let alone be capable of under-standing it."[8]

If this can be assumed, *Death of a Salesman* takes on the high seriousness of Greek tragedy. Structurally, it is as taut as *Oedipus*; there are no digressions, and Willy Loman marches inexorably from his entering, "It's all right. I came back," to his doom. Given the circumstances, he cannot behave other than as he does. Even the manner of his death follows the classic pattern of keeping violence offstage, while the "Requiem" section functions in the manner of a Greek chorus. Miller developed the choral aspect more com-pletely in *A View from the Bridge*, and in both plays, it serves the same purpose as in classic drama—precluding sentimentality by bring-ing in an outside, objective view of the action.

[7]Zygmunt Adamczewski, *The Tragic Protest* (The Hague: Martinus Nijhoff, 1963), p. 192. Others who have commented on this question are: George de Schweinitz, *Death of a Salesman*: A Note on Epic and Tragedy," *Western Humanities Review* 14 (Winter 1960), 91–96; M. W. Steinberg, "Arthur Miller and the Idea of Modern Tragedy," *Dalhousie Review* XL, 329–40; Alvin Whitley, "Arthur Miller: An Attempt at Modern Tragedy," *Transactions of the Wisconsin Academy of Sciences, Arts and Letters* 42 (1953), 257–62.

[8]Arthur Miller, "Tragedy and the Common Man," in *The Theatre Essays of Arthur Miller*, ed. Robert H. Martin (New York: Viking, 1978), pp. 3–4.

Death of a Salesman departs from classic tradition in at least three areas too important to dismiss from consideration: subject, language, and character. According to Aristotelian standards, the subject matter is hardly of the proper magnitude; one might feel pity for Willy Loman but not the awesome terror that produces catharsis. Neither the life nor the death of an unknown and misguided salesman has an effect on the larger world which will continue on its way without interruption or change, without, indeed, even pausing to notice. The proposition that every life is important and that it is symbolic of the larger society may be valid, but it is a twentieth-century concept, not part of the classic view that the subject must have cosmic consequences.

Miller's dialogue, too, suffers when placed beside the classic model. While the poetic form is no longer regarded as essential to tragedy, the ambiguity of its language usually incorporates a range of meanings applicable (if in different terms) to many ages and cultures. Except for the "Requiem" section, the words in *Death of a Salesman* are seldom applicable beyond the immediate situation, do not echo with great truths, and are, in fact, frequently banal:

> *Willy:* I'll start out in the morning. Maybe I'll
> feel better in the morning. (She is taking off
> his shoes) These goddam arch supports are
> killing me.
> *Linda:* Take an aspirin. Should I get you an
> aspirin? It'll soothe you.[9]

Miller defended his usage on the ground that Willy himself is inarticulate, and it is true that this very quality establishes the main point of the play. Individual speeches may not be pithy aphorisms or important in themselves, but the aggregate creates a strong link between the life of Willy Loman and any other life that is circumscribed by ordinary, everyday events. True, the words may seem inadequate when read in the library, but Miller is writing for the stage where the dialogue counts less than the context within which it is spoken and the situation shown by the visual picture. Elements such as the relationships of characters or the very tone of the actor's voice are needed to produce the total experience. Miller

[9]Arthur Miller, *Death of a Salesman* (New York: Viking, 1949), pp. 13–14. All further textual references are to this edition.

has not written poetry in the traditional literary sense; what he has done, instead, is to use language in combination with all the theatrical resources at his command, to provide a poetic experience in the playhouse.

The most striking departure from classic tragedy is in the character of the protagonist. Willy Loman is light years away from Oedipus in concept and in presentation: he is not of noble birth, he is not a leader of men, he has little self-knowledge, he achieves no insight, and his moral values are deplorable. His sole "heroic" quality is his integrity. His principles may be unconscious and built on fallacies, but he believes in them, practices them, and, finally, dies for them. Integrity is a noble quality, but it is not enough to put him on equal footing with the heroes of the past, and Miller has claimed a need for a redefinition of "hero":

> ... his stature as a hero is not so utterly dependent upon his rank that the corner grocer cannot outdistance him as a tragic figure—providing, of course, that the grocer's career engages the issues of, for instance, the survival of the race, the relationships of man to God—the questions, in short, whose answers define humanity and the right way to live so that the world is a home, instead of a battleground or a fog in which disembodied spirits pass each other in an endless twilight.[10]

Such a change of definition risks a certain loss of meaning and suggests that the very concept of hero has changed. Yet audiences still respond to Oedipus, Hamlet, Lear, and Othello—not because of their bloodlines or their social preeminence, not even because of their achievements, but because there is a recognized kinship with their acceptance of responsibility, their personal insight and their morality—in short, with their humanity. Even in today's judgment they represent the best of the species, imperfect but with immense possibilities. Willy, on the other hand, is not worse than most men nor is he noticeably better, and his fall is not from such a height that it shatters our complacency; rather, it is a fate neither remarkable nor remarked. The power of the work does not derive from admiration of what a person might be but from the awareness of what a person is, a concept that bears so little resemblance to that of the past that it might be preferable to give it another

---

[10]Arthur Miller, Introduction to *Collected Plays* (New York: Viking, 1957), p. 145.

name entirely than to try and reconcile the differences under a single term.

Some writers have resolved the question by classifying the play as a domestic tragedy.[11] Certainly, in subject matter, characters, language, and setting it matches this tradition more closely than it does the classic. Yet here, too, a substantial departure prevents a simple classification, for domestic tragedy, first popularized by *The London Merchant* (1730), is separated from the classical tradition by more than the reduced social status of its characters. Its pattern leads toward melodrama, relying on emotion rather than solemn grandeur for its impact. In domestic tragedies, the actions of the ordinary person do not have the far-reaching consequences that make those of the great leader intrinsically interesting, but an emotional identification with the character makes it—at least during the performance time—equally impressive.

The early domestic tragedies were in the nature of an antidote to the elevated tradition which had come to substitute empty rhetoric for impassioned poetry, but the use of emotion to arouse the "sensibilities" soon became an end in itself. As it developed through the eighteenth-century *Fatal Curiosity* and the romanticized nineteenth-century *East Lynne* to the film *Love Story*, the protagonist became a victim as the focus of this genre changed, moving from an emphasis on character to an emphasis on events that produced painful ordeals. Often, in a domestic tragedy, the suffering is unmerited—coincidence, misunderstanding, or chance brings disaster, and the success of the work is gauged by the amount of emotion it arouses. Despite its lack of substance (which kept it from consideration as a serious form of art), it has been one of the most popular genres in the theater.

Miller, however, turns away from melodrama and easily aroused tears and pays his protagonist the highest respect by taking him seriously. Willy Loman has the soul of a tragic hero trapped in the body and mind of an ordinary man. Externally, his status is negligible, but as a member of the human race, he represents a part of all people, and his fate brings no brief, superficial reaction in the theater but a lasting impression "too deep for tears."

Domestic tragedy also led to another path quite apart from melodrama when it became a mode for stating social problems. It

[11]Many have commented on this, notably John Gassner, *Form and Idea in Modern Theatre* (New York: Dryden, 1956).

is possible to read *Death of a Salesman* as a continuation of the line that began with Ibsen and includes Augier, Brieux, Shaw, Galsworthy, and Odets; a number of studies have approached it from this angle.[12] It is a tempting classification: like Ibsen's John Gabriel Borkman, Loman has been cast out of the mainstream; like Elmer Rice's Mr. Zero, he is a small cog in a large machine, driven to desperation by impersonal events; like Clifford Odets' Lefty, he can be seen as one of the oppressed. The high city buildings looming over his property are visible evidence of antagonistic powers; they have cut off the source of light and life, killed the trees, and prevented future growth. Willy himself is outdated, redundant; his heroes are his independent brother, Ben, who boasts, "When I went into the jungle, I was seventeen. When I walked out I was twenty-one. And, by God, I was rich!" (p. 52), and the perfect salesman, Dave Singleman, drumming up merchandise in thirty-one states by staying in his hotel room, where he would "put on his green velvet slippers—I'll never forget—and pick up his phone and call the buyers, and without ever leaving his room, at the age of eighty-four, he made his living." (p. 81). They are figures from the past, and Willy's attempts to mold himself into their likeness must fail in a world where product takes precedence over personality. It is easy to see him as a victim of the illusive American dream that cruelly held out a promise while denying the opportunity of fulfillment.[13]

Loman, however, is not an innocent destroyed by a corrupt society but a man who gradually destroys himself through ignorance and blindness, placing his trust in false values that must inevitably crumble. The evil is not in external forces—not in

[12]See Kenneth Allsop, "A Conversation with Arthur Miller," *Encounter* XIII, 1 (July 1959), 58–60; Winifred L. Dusenbury, "Personal Failure" in *The Theme of Loneliness in Modern American Drama* (Gainesville, Fla.: University of Florida, 1960), pp. 8–37; Eric Mottram, "Arthur Miller: The Development of a Political Dramatist in America," in *American Theatre*, ed. John Russell Brown and Bernard Harris, Stratford-upon-Avon series, no. 10 (London: Edward Arnold, 1967), pp. 127–161.

[13]See Chester E. Eisinger, "Focus on Arthur Miller's *Death of a Salesman*: The Wrong Dream," in *American Dream's American Nightmares*, ed. David Madden (Carbondale, Ill.: University of Southern Illinois, 1970), pp. 165–74; Alfred E. Ferguson, "The Tragedy of the American Dream in *Death of a Salesman*," *Thought* 53 (March 1978), 83–98; William Heyen, "Arthur Miller's *Death of a Salesman* and The American Dream," in *Amerikanisches Drama und Theater im 10. Jahrhundert* (Gottingen: Vandenhoek and Ruprecht, 1975), pp. 192–221.

Howard who is merely a catalytic agent when he fires Willy, not in Charley, who practices a stolid morality without preaching it, not even in the impersonal growth of an industrialized culture. It is in Willy himself and in every other character as part of the human condition.

Miller is not sentimental about his characters, but he has too much compassion to present them as caricatures. Even Howard, for all his insensitivity to Willy's needs, is not a vicious exploiter of the working class but an ironic parallel to Willy himself, an ordinary man who is concerned with his livelihood, takes pleasure in ordinary things, and has great pride in his offspring. Only the conditions are different: Howard is young and prosperous; the spectre of old age, weakened powers, and poverty are hidden in the future. Miller's juxtaposition of the two men allows us to see the parallel and, simultaneously, to see Howard as a human being rather than the instrument of a hostile society.

The values of the individual life, then, not of society in general, are Miller's concern in another tradition that leads back to the medieval morality play. There are, of course, obvious differences in characterization and purpose, but the deep structure of *Death of a Salesman* is remarkably similar to that of *Everyman*. One by one the things Willy Loman cherishes fall away, leaving only Good Deeds to accompany him to the grave. He stands as an object lesson in morality, for in spite of his sense of responsibility ("He works for a company thirty-six years this March" p. 56), his love for his wife ("On the road—on the road I want to grab you sometimes and just kiss the life out of you" p. 38), and his best efforts for his son ("I never in my life told him anything but decent things" p. 41), his lack of adherence to the basic standards of right and wrong leads him to disaster.

Death of a Salesman may, in part, be drawn from the morality tradition, but the relationship is not one-to-one, for Miller departs from it in the important areas of character and purpose. Willy is not Everyman. Although a number of critics have seen him in this light,[14] it is a more cynical view than the play warrants, and Miller denies it vehemently:

[14]See William B. Dillingham, "Arthur Miller and the Loss of Conscience," *Emory University Quarterly* 16 (Spring 1960), 40–50; Helen M. McMahon, "Arthur Miller's Common Man: The Problem of Realistic and Mythic," *Drama and Theatre* 10 (1972), 128–33; William Wiegand, "Arthur Miller and the Man Who Knows," *Western Review* 21 (Winter 1957), 85–103.

It is obvious that Willy *can't* be an average American man, at least from one point of view; he kills himself. That's a rare thing in society, although it is more common than one could wish, and it's beside the point. As a matter of fact, the standard of "averageness" is not valid. It neither tells whether the character is a truthful character as a character, or a valid one. . . . I didn't write *Death of a Salesman* to announce some new American man, or an old American man. Willy Loman is, I think, a person who embodies in himself some of the terrible conflicts running through the streets of America today.[15]

He is not Everyman but *Lo*man—one who, as Biff points out, is "a dime a dozen," who accepts the world without question and never seeks to better it, who reacts without thought, who substitutes dreams for knowledge, and who is necessarily self-centered because unanalyzed feelings are his sole touchstone to existence.

Moreover, the play is not a didactic teaching instrument; it is an observation of the behavior of humans. We may draw our own conclusions in whatever terms we choose, for Miller is not preaching a simple lesson on the ways of righteousness. The play does not end with Willy's death, and the future, as represented by Biff and Happy, may be bleak, but it is not hopeless, for Biff, at least, has been freed from the web of falsehood that warped his early years and destroyed his father.

Of all the traditions from which *Death of a Salesman* is drawn, the most marked in the theater, perhaps, is the stylistic combination of realism and impressionism.[16] Miller's ability to reconcile two normally antithetic types of expression into a coherent entity gives him the advantages of both. Putting aside the philosophic question of "reality," the theatrical model is a style developed in the nineteenth century partly as a result of technological advances that developed the machinery to reflect the everyday world in mirror-

[15]Arthur Miller, "Morality and Modern Drama" in *The Theatre Essays of Arthur Miller*, p. 199.

[16]For a thorough description of the design and concepts of the visual staging, see Jo Mielziner, *Designing for the Theatre* (New York: Atheneum, 1965). For other views, see Louis Broussard, *American Drama: Contemporary Allegory from Eugene O'Neill to Tennessee Williams* (Norman, Oklahoma: University of Oklahoma, 1963), pp. 117–20; Fred Hunter, "The Value of Time in Modern Drama" *Journal of Aesthetics and Art Criticism* 16 (1957), 194–201; Raymond Williams, "The Realism of Arthur Miller," *Critical Quarterly* 1 (1959), 140–49.

like terms, partly from the cultural, social, and artistic forces undergoing change at the same time.

The scenes in *Death of a Salesman* that take place in the present are a realistic portrayal of Loman's life. Willy strikes a familiar chord with, "Once in my life, I would like to own something outright before it's broken! I'm always in a race with the junk-yard!" (p. 73) The daily actions of drinking coffee, mending stockings, or washing the car are meticulously shown. Even when his life is pressing to a close, the sequence of events is told through small, deceptively ordinary scenes: a restaurant, a home, a quarrel, a reconciliation.

Interlocked with this tradition is an anti-realism, most closely associated with the impressionistic/expressionistic theater that also began toward the end of the nineteenth century, curiously enough, also partially a result of theatrical technology. The control of lighting afforded by the use of electricity allowed the playwright to focus attention on any area of the stage, to alter the tone visually, and to have almost unlimited freedom of internal time. This freedom, carried further with the invention of the cinema camera, profoundly altered the patterns of drama.

Miller does not write in the poetic vein of Maeterlinck or Strindberg, but he does refocus the attention abruptly, alter tone, and distort normal time as they do. The three elements work simultaneously: in the midst of an ordinary conversation, Willy's long-dead brother Ben appears, and the tone shifts from Happy's prosaic "I'm getting married, Pop, don't forget it. I'm changing everything. I'm gonna run that department before the year is up," (pp. 133–134) to Ben's ominous, "The jungle is dark but full of diamonds, Willy." This is perfectly appropriate and not in the least distracting, for the effectiveness of the play requires such a sudden alteration in time and place.

Dramatic license has always allowed for liberty in these matters. The two "unities" of time and place have seldom been taken seriously by English playwrights; Shakespeare's violations of the classic "rules" may have been censured by neoclassic critics, but audiences were never disturbed by a move from Alexandria to Rome or the compression of sixteen years into a choral interlude. The development of the action through flashback or dream goes back at least as far as Laura Keene's *Camille* (c. 1860) which tried to avoid the charge of immorality by making the story of the un-happy Marguerite Gauthier a dream from which she awakened with a resolution to be a good girl henceforth. This kind of time warp is relatively simple, for it is as sequential in itself as the action that frames it, and it has been a common device in film almost since the beginning.

Miller's manipulation of the time factor is somewhat different, as the original title of the play, *The Inside of His Head*, indicates. Memory plays an important part in the action, but it is memory in a psychological or Proustian fashion, rather than the kind Tennessee Williams uses in *The Glass Menagerie*. In Miller's usage, an incident or a word in the present suddenly conjures up the memory of a related experience that forwards, or is part of, the action. In real life, such memories are usually momentary flashes, clustering sensory, emotional, and/or intellectual experiences together in a brief and intense realization; because the drama of necessity proceeds forward in time, Miller has had to create scenes that are not instantaneous perceptions; they must move ahead while carrying enough information to make a point. The memory episodes are neither sequential with each other nor do they form a single cohesive unit, but they are essential to the action. Willy's mind goes from present to past to present without the other characters noticing anything more than a temporary silence, a nonsequitur of speech or a minor memory lapse too slight to be alarming. The audience, however, sees the operation of Loman's mind unfolding before them in a manner related to similar experiences of their own and entirely comprehensible in a post-Freudian society.

The molding of inner and outer experience into a combination of the matter-of-fact and the matter-of-fancy was a new mode in 1949. Earlier playwrights had questioned "reality" (Pirandello), created their own (Maeterlinck, Kaiser), or denied the existence of a division between that of the stage and that of the audience (Brecht). Later playwrights, like Albee and Stoppard, have adapted Miller's approach to their own purposes, but in its first presentation, *Death of a Salesman* opened an area that had not previously been explored.

Miller's skillful use of tradition and originality gives *Death of a Salesman* a respectable place in American drama, but if this were all there were to the play, it would merely be an example of excellent craftsmanship. What gives the work its importance is what Miller has to say. In clear, concise twentieth-century terms, he asks the question that has plagued our species since we were first able to formulate it: what is man all about? what is this featherless biped who is never satisfied, who, having been given life, reaches for immortality? The question is subsumed by an assumption of such temerity that the heavens must ring with laughter at its arrogance—the assumption that humanity is necessary to the universe. Outrageous enough in the beginning, it has expanded through the centuries to include more than just the royal descendants of gods or the movers and shakers of early societies. In the twentieth century, it includes every member of the human race and presupposes that each person, whether standing on the bridge directing the course of the ship or stoking coal in the darkness below the waterline, is indispensable to the community—and that each community is a microcosm of the universe. Speaking with the voice of his own time, Miller has enlarged Donne's "each man's death diminishes me" to an insistence that every human being is worthy of consideration and respect, that, doer or dreamer, "Attention must be paid. . ."

Death of a Salesman

Dennis Welland

The role of Willy Loman was created by Lee J. Cobb in Elia Kazan's Broadway production of 1949. When the London production opened five months later the part was played by Paul Muni. This gratuitous piece of historical information highlights conveniently a controversy about the play that still persists and illustrates the stamp that an actor's interpretation can leave on a drama. Looking back on the notices of these first productions one could be forgiven for thinking that there were two plays, the American *Death of a Salesman* and the British.

British reviewers, such as Harold Hobson, who had seen both actors in the role emphasised the radical differences between the two interpretations:

> Mr. Cobb's Loman was a man rejoicing in his enormous vitality, and quite unaware of his essential uselessness, the realisation of which came upon him at the end as a shattering and incomprehensible paradox. Mr. Muni's performance, on the other hand, was that of a sad little chap beaten from the start, pushed around by life and his fellows, pathetically incompetent, touching and exasperating by turns. Mr. Cobb took the play along with splendid drive, but hardly ever unsealed the springs of pity. Mr. Muni was frequently moving, but occasionally became a bore.[1]

In 1949 Hobson had been a little more sympathetic, observing that "on at least five occasions Mr. Muni brings the entire audience close to tears" and "in the supreme moments of his performance Mr. Muni could not be surpassed." To Philip Hope-Wallace in New York the play had seemed "something comparable

Dennis Welland, *Miller: A Study of His Plays*, (London: Eyre Methuen, 1979), pp. 36–53. Copyright © 1979 by Dennis Welland. Reprinted by permission of the author and publisher.

[1]Harold Hobson, *The Theatre Now* (1953), p. 125. The quotation that follows this is from his *Sunday Times* review.

to an American *King Lear*" but comparison with the London production made him "regretfully withdraw" this: unlike Cobb, Muni did not seem to feel that it was Willy's "illusion (even as Lear's illusion of kingship) which made him big by his own lights and makes his fall tragic." Yet, as Audrey Williamson was to point out, "Willy's 'success' is a mirage that deceives no one but himself and Muni's crushed nervousness had a poignant reality."[2]

Muni was already popular in England for stage and screen performances. *The Times* captioned its photograph of the play "Mr. Muni's Return" and several reviews approached it primarily as a vehicle for him. For J.C. Trewin, indeed, Muni was the play's only redeeming feature: his review read, in its entirety:

> *Death of a Salesman*, Arthur Miller's American play at the Phoenix, was almost the death of a critic. Happily, Paul Muni is in the cast to play the little salesman with a pathetic belief in this worthless son, and his vigour and humanity help to relieve an evening that is otherwise tangled, pretentious, and dull. It is, however, a commercial success.[3]

This is out of key with most other British reviews only in its hostility in the play: Trewin's emphasis on "the little salesman" as a pathetic figure was echoed by many others. The British *Death of a Salesman* established itself as a moving story of human failure, the self-destruction of a little man; the American is an examination of the impact on an ordinary, though not necessarily little, salesman of a national success-ethic. "The American Dream" was a phrase less current in Britain in the 1940s than it has since become. It envisages a society in which success through his own efforts is still as available to the ordinary man as it was in the expansive, pioneering days of the last century; looking back nostalgically to the simpler, homely values of those days, it also looks forward to the possibility of grasping opportunity with equal vigour in modern circumstances so that sturdy, independent enterprise will be rewarded by a sense of achievement, improved living conditions for the individual and his family, and, in all probability,

---

[2]Philip Hope-Wallace reviewed it in *The Manchester Guardian* on 30 July 1949 and *Time and Tide* 6 August; Audrey Williamson wrote on it in *Theatre of Two Decades* (London, Rockliff, 1951).

[3]*Drama* (Winter, 1949), p. 8. Trewin also reviewed it in *The Illustrated London News*, 27 August 1949.

affluence. An audience nourished on such beliefs would naturally
be alert to evidence of them in Willy's aspirations and would be
sympathetic to his dismay at a changing world in which they seem
no longer capable of realisation. Only one or two British reviewers, however, saw Willy as essentially American, though to a
number he was, in the words of *Theatre World*, " 'Everyman' once
again, in our day and generation, more blind than ever to the real
spiritual values of life." Of those who disposed to see it as a
morality play none (perhaps surprisingly) thought of it as a Marxist
or even a left-wing morality, yet in New York, of course, those tags
were much more readily applied.

Differing national attitudes toward communism at that time
might explain this. The name of Elia Kazan was less well-known
here than it is now, and less well-known than in America; both he
and Lee J. Cobb had been in the original cast of the 1935 Group
Theater production of Clifford Odets's *Waiting for Lefty*, a circum-
stance which, coupled with Miller's connection with the Federal
Theater Project, may have predisposed some Americans to expect
a play more redolent of the thirties than would an English audience. Audrey Williamson was to recall that Kazan and Cobb had
both been in the 1938 London production of Odets's *Golden Boy*;
she had evidently been much impressed by that play and by the
work of the Group Theater, but no London reviewer in 1949 made
this connection. The Muni reading could have lent itself to the
anti-capitalist emphasis so often put on the play, but it does not
seem to have done so: Hobson's "sad little chap" is "pushed
around by life and his fellows," not by forces more sinister.

One critic's description of it as "a deeply understanding study of
a once happy family torn to pieces by forces outside its comprehension"[4] is typical. *The Times* felt that "this massive and relentless
play" falls into two halves, of which the first shows "the straits in
which an unnatural civilisation places natural man," and "the
second, and much better, half of the play" concentrates on the
father/son relationship with a sense of the tragic which "amply
makes up for the overwhelming accumulation of detail with which
the dramatist prepares for it." The word to which most British
reviewers sooner or later had recourse was "moving," but they
were moved emotionally, not politically.

[4]Eric Keown, *Punch*, 10 August 1949.

Its 742 New York performances immediately put it into the *Burns Mantle Yearbook* list of the fifty longest recorded Broadway runs (including musicals) and it remained in that list until 1960. Such success did not prevent—indeed, perhaps invited—hostility, and the question which has always bedevilled discussion of *Death of a Salesman* was quickly raised: is it a tragedy? Eric Bentley, abroad when it opened in February 1949, attacked it on his return, hitting hard at everything from the lighting to the language, but especially at what he saw as the play's conflicting aims:

> The "tragedy" destroys the social drama; the social drama keeps the "tragedy" from having a genuinely tragic stature. By this last remark I mean that the theme of this social drama, as of most others, is *the little man as victim*. The theme arouses pity but no terror. Man is here too little and too passive to play the tragic hero.
> More important even than this, the tragedy and the social drama actually conflict. The tragic catharsis reconciles us to, or persuades us to disregard, precisely those material conditions which the social drama calls our attention to . . . Or is Mr. Miller a "tragic" artist who without knowing it has been confused by Marxism?[5]

Exactly the reverse hypothesis was advanced by Eleanor Clark in *Partisan Review*; she saw Miller as a Marxist who had been confused by tragedy:

> It is, of course, the capitalist system that has done Willy in; the scene in which he is brutally fired after some forty years with the firm comes straight from the party-line literature of the thirties, and the idea emerges lucidly enough through all the confused motivations of the play that it is our particular form of money economy that has bred the absurdly false ideals of both father and sons. It emerges, however, like a succession of shots from a duck-blind. Immediately after every crack the playwright withdraws behind an air of pseudo-universality, and hurries to present some cruelty or misfortune due either to Willy's own weakness, as when he refuses a friend's offer of a job after he has been fired, or gratuitously from some other source, as in the quite unbelievable scene of the two sons walking out on their father in the restaurant.[6]

The whole play, for Miss Clark, is characterised by "an intellectual

[5]*Theatre Arts*, November 1949, p. 13.

[6]Eleanor Clark, "Death of a Salesman," *Partisan Review*, 16 (1949), 632; reprinted in *Two Modern Tragedies*, ed. John D. Hurrell (New York: Scribner's, 1961), pp. 61–64.

muddle and a lack of candor that regardless of Mr. Miller's conscious intent are the main earmark of contemporary fellow-travelling. What used to be a roar has become a whine."

At about the time of the play's opening, Miller himself, interviewed by *The New York Times*, stressed the tragic intention:

> The tragic feeling is evoked in us when we are in the presence of a character who is ready to lay down his life, if need be, to secure one thing—his sense of personal dignity.[7]

Important as this idea is in Miller's later plays, it was confusing when associated with *Death of a Salesman*, for critics were quick to point out what the play itself demonstrated—that Willy Loman's sense of personal dignity was too precariously based to give him heroic stature. Since then it has become tediously conventional for the writers of books surveying modern drama to praise the play's social realism but hurriedly to add that, of course, it falls short of tragedy and is therefore disqualified as a "great play." (This complaint is usually associated with strictures on its unpoetic use of language.)

What is irritating about such criticism is its assured conviction that the mixture of social drama and tragedy is unintentional, and its implication, that, if Miller had only been clear-minded enough to concentrate on one or the other, a better play would have resulted. Eric Bentley is perfectly right to see it as a play about "the little man as victim," but less right when he seems to prefer the little man to be a victim of only one thing, and to assume that a "social drama" must be a socialist drama. The Marxist plays of Clifford Odets had rarely communicated a sense of the complex density of the society they criticised, and merely to show the little man as the victim of capitalist big business would, in 1949, have been to repeat what Elmer Rice had done in *The Adding Machine* twenty-six years earlier.

The evidence for a Marxist interpretation of *Death of a Salesman* is not very impressive. The scene in which Willy, seeking a change of job, is unceremoniously dismissed can hardly have been intended as the indictment of capitalism that Miss Clark thinks it. Theatrically it is a moving, even painful, scene, but it engenders a mixture of pity and exasperation rather than the indignation that

---

[7]*"Death of a Salesman:* Miller Discusses Writing the Play," *New York Times*, February 6, 1949, II, 1:5.

we would expect of "party-line literature." Willy's behaviour is not calculated to enhance his or our sense of his personal dignity; even as we pity him for his despairing reduction of the wage he will settle for, we are exasperated by his inability to see that, by his obtuse mishandling of Howard, he is throwing away any chance he may have. The central irony of this scene resides in the discrepancy between Howard and our preconceived idea of the capitalist tycoon. This is no ruthless executive callously firing the trusted employee from calculated mercenary motives: it is the "nice guy" forced into a situation that he doesn't know how to handle "nicely" and consequently only making the ugliness of it worse. It is one little man being fired by another little man, Willy being fired by a younger Willy.

Howard's callousness is occasioned less by his business acumen than by his absorption in his personal life. The tape-recorder serves two purposes in the scene: when Willy stumbles against it and sets it accidentally into motion it precipitates an hysterical breakdown that symbolises the central theme of the play in Willy's horror at his inability to switch it off—to switch off the recorded past. Whether the past is that of his own sons recorded on his memory and conscience, or that of Howard's son recorded on a mechanical instrument, it is the past, more than capitalism, of which Willy is always the victim. The machine also provides a means of dramatising Howard's ingenuous pride in his children. They are far more real to him than is the memory of his father to which Willy constantly appeals, and his pride in their prowess and in their affection for him obliterates any understanding of Willy's plight, exactly as Willy's pride in his own sons has blinded him to any recognition of the worth of Bernard. This point is emphasised by Howard's automatic question, "Why don't your sons give you a hand?" and by the immediate introduction of the Ben-*motif* as a further reproach to Willy's vacillatory sentimentality.

Moreover, this memory-sequence dissolves into the actuality of Charley's office, where a successful Bernard on his way to professional and social triumphs in Washington unintentionally prompts Willy into another orgy of envious recrimination at everybody except himself. The irony set in motion in Howard's office culminates in Charley's, for it is Charley, not Howard, who is the nearest thing to the big business-man in this play, and yet Charley is the only person who offers Willy any positive help. The money he advances him and the employment he offers have no strings

attached: Willy's acceptance of the one and rejection of the other is
the outcome of a very curious sense of personal dignity, but there
is no mistaking the truth of his exit line: "Charley, you're the only
friend I got. Isn't that a remarkable thing?"

It is remarkable to Willy not only because he has never had any
time for Charley, but because Charley is the exact antithesis of
himself. To describe Charley as the Horatio to Willy's Hamlet (as
at least one critic has done) is to put it too romantically, but the
antithesis is clearly and succinctly drawn by Willy's exchange with
Charley over Bernard's success:

> *Willy:* And you never told him what to do, did you? You
> never took any interest in him.
> *Charley:* My salvation is that I never took any interest in
> anything. There's some money— fifty dollars. I got
> an accountant inside. (p. 75)*

Charley the successful business-man is the only person who
understands Willy the failed salesman, but he understands him in a
wholly unsentimental way quite different from the "interest" that
is Willy's more characteristic response. He will help Willy with
a job or with money, but he will not tell him what to do; he expects
Willy, like Bernard, to make his own choice. Having subordinated
sentiment to business efficiency all his life, Charley can allow his
feelings to come through at Willy's funeral, and his final speech,
"Nobody dast blame this man . . . ," though it is not the moral of
the play, ought to have made unnecessary Miller's prefatory
disavowal of any intended arraignment of big business.

This tacit acceptance of business as long as it is kept distinct
from sentiment is not a noticeably Marxist position. Yet Miller
does not seem to intend a criticism of Howard for dismissing Willy
("when a man gets old you fire him, you have to, he can't do the
work"): but he contrives that dismissal so as to show Howard in as
un-business-like a light as possible. The way in which Lawrence
Newman is fired in Miller's novel *Focus*, on far more slender
grounds, makes a marked contrast to this scene. Newman is being
efficiently sacrificed to business efficiency where Willy, himself a
bungler, is being dismissed by a man no better than himself. To

*Unless otherwise indicated, all page references following quotations from
Death of a Salesman relate to the Penguin edition, published in Harmondsworth,
England, 1961.

this extent we sympathise with Willy's dilemma, but our respect is
not given to either party, and the dramatic impact of this scene,
properly played, ought to be one of inevitability—neither has any
real alternative—and of littleness—neither is himself big enough
to see the other, or to transcend his own sentimentality.

Even Willy's eulogy of old Dave Singleman, who "was eighty-
four years old, and he'd drummed merchandise in thirty-one
states" and who "died the death of a salesman," has to be seen, for
all its subdued eloquence, in this light. Strategically placed in this
key scene, it constitutes a criticism of Willy in its garrulous ir-
relevance to his situation, and at the same time it is a condemnation of Howard for his failure to grasp its significance for Willy. Yet
how little even this myth really means to Willy is ironically under-
lined in the next scene, when, tempted by Ben's offer of Alaskan
wealth, he needs to be reminded of it by Linda:

> *Ben:* What are you building? Lay your hand on it.
>   Where is it?
> *Willy (hesitantly):* That's true, Linda, there's nothing.
> *Linda:* Why? *(To Ben:)* There's a man eighty-four years
>   old . . .
> *Willy:* That's right, Ben, that's right. When I look at that
>   man I say, what is there to worry about? (p. 67)

Ben's contemptuous "Bah!" is well-merited by the aura that this
has of a piece of family folk-lore, a germ of Willy's self-deception to
which Linda has been so repeatedly exposed that she has caught
the infection worse than he has.

Conflicting with the salesman-ideal of success in a capitalist-
commercial society, there is the pioneer-ideal of success in the
"great outdoors," represented by Willy not only in the person of
Ben but in the idealised race-memory of the challenge of the
frontier, embodied in his father, who drove a waggon-team right
across the country selling flutes. There is also the popular image of
success through sporting prowess: Biff the hero of the football
field is another dream whereby Willy seeks his own identity.
Neither of these is fully explored here; rather are they introduced
as stereotypes to which the popular imagination always responds.
Miller is very careful to insist on all these sets of ideals as *Willy's*.
He deliberately provides no external documentation of Willy's
memories of his own earlier success as a salesman. We hear of it
only from Willy himself and, with less conviction, from Linda;
Howard disputes it and Charley never offers any corroborative

evidence. Similarly even the image of his waggon-driving father is something second-hand, not part of his own memory, but something he has been told of by Ben, who himself is not a character, but a creation of Willy's fancy. The title for the play was first to have been *The Inside of His Head*, a conception which deliberately precludes the external criteria required by tragedy. Tragedy also requires of its hero a final recognition of which, by his very nature, as well as by the nature of the play, Willy Loman is incapable.

Tragedy implies values; and to the repeated complaint that Willy has no values, Miller has replied in these terms:

> The trouble with Willy Loman is that he has tremendously powerful ideals. We're not accustomed to speaking of ideals in his terms; but, if Willy Loman, for instance, had not had a very profound sense that his life as lived had left him hollow, he would have died contentedly polishing his car on some Sunday afternoon at a ripe old age. The fact is he has values. The fact that they cannot be realized is what is driving him mad—just as, unfortunately, it's driving a lot of other people mad. The truly valueless man, a man without ideals, is always perfectly at home anywhere.

Later in the same piece, however, Miller defined his aim in the play as being "to set forth what happens when a man does not have a grip on the forces of life and has no sense of values which will lead him to that kind of a grip."[8] The two statements are not, as some critics argue, contradictory. They are in fact reconciled by Biff's epitaph on his father: "He had the wrong dreams. All, all wrong." Charley's reply amounts to little more than a plea in mitigation: Willy *had* to dream. The only person who challenges Biff's verdict is Happy, who is by this stage of the play thoroughly discredited; and Willy's suicide itself implies some recognition, even though limited, of his wrong values.

Willy's inability to be "always perfectly at home anywhere" proves in Miller's terms that he is not "the truly valueless man." Yet to be at home in the world is Willy's greatest desire; it is not an unworthy one, but it is certainly not the aspiration of a tragic hero.

In *Death of a Salesman* the difficulties in "making of the outside world a home" are borne in on the spectator in the theatre by the

[8]*Tulane Drama Review* II (May, 1958), pp. 63–9. The passage quoted should be compared with the parallel passage at the foot of p. 34 in *Collected Plays*.

set itself. In *All My Sons* the action takes place in "the back yard of the Keller home ... hedged on right and left by tall, closely planted poplars which lend the yard a secluded atmosphere." This represents effectively Joe Keller's success in cocooning himself in a home cut off from the outside world, the inexorable intrusion of which is the play's main theme. Willy Loman cannot thus isolate himself domestically. Less successful and less affluent than Keller, he cannot live secludedly "in the outskirts of an American town" but, as the light comes up on the set, "we see a solid vault of apartment houses around the small, fragile-seeming home" and of these we are kept relentlessly aware until the final curtain. The threatening pressures of the outside world will intensify the fragility of that home throughout the play until eventually they destroy it completely: one of those pressures is embodied in the difficulties, all too familiar in the modern world, of home-ownership in the face of increasing property-values. The point is made, almost over-neatly, by Linda's last words as the play ends: "I made the last payment on the house today. Today, dear. And there'll be nobody home. We're free and clear. We're free. We're free."

The irony and pathos of those lines are prepared for throughout the play not only by the action but visually as well. The house is as much a character in the play as the farmhouse had been in Eugene O'Neill's *Desire under the Elms* in 1924, and Miller adapted to his own ends that stage-set of the house in cross-section seen in its external surroundings. This "exploded house" set which keeps the whole interior continuously on display mirrors the family combustion that came more and more to dominate the American theatre, and is peculiarly suited to this dramatic idiom. Its stylised unnaturalness reminds us that we are in a theatre—we can see actions happening simultaneously, and often quite independently, in two places—while its revelatory intimacy and disruption of privacy ensure our engagement in the action. We can be within and without simultaneously.

In the theatre Willy Loman's house is dwarfed by the omnipresence of the towering apartment houses all round it which, like O'Neill's elms, are a visual equivalent to the terrible claustrophobia of the play's theme. In a burst of misplaced agrarian escapism Willy goes out with a flashlight to sow the seeds that he has somehow never found time to plant before. On a bare stage this might seem insufferably allegorical: with the setting Miller demands, this consideration is overwhelmed by the painful grotesqueness of the situation. Nothing brings out more sharply the pathetic ineffectualness and bewilderment and littleness of the man than this scene, and the setting gives an added dimension to his otherwise petulant explosion: "Where the hell is that seed? You can't see nothing out here. They boxed in the whole goddam neighborhood." (p. 101)

The walls to which Willy is a prisoner are less tangible than any of brick and stone, and yet by keeping us visually aware of those physical walls Miller simultaneously suggests the metaphysical walls as well. As the action of the play, taking place in Willy's mind, with effortless fluidity breaks through the walls of the stage house, the strength of the walls of his neurosis is accentuated. In the same way, in *Focus*, Lawrence Newman (whose place of work is the Wall Street district) had sat in a glass-walled private office, a prisoner to inner terrors of which the transparent walls make him and us the more conscious.

It is, in short, a mistake to apply too strictly to *Death of a Salesman* the standards of realism by which the earlier plays ask to be judged. That we are never told the nature of the merchandise Willy sells or the surnames of any other characters other than the Lomans is not a failure of the realistic method. Miller's own answer, "When asked what Willy was selling . . . I could only reply, 'Himself' "—is fair enough; these details are not necessary to a play that is nearer to expressionism than to realism.

In notices of the original production praise for Jo Mielziner's set was more general than for the structure of the play which puzzled many reviewers. One thought "The episodic time-switching and place-switching" was a concession to audiences who really preferred the cinema; another sneered that "it makes for easy play writing: problems of construction vanish." More sympathetically a third wrote "Usually I dislike seeing the whole of a house laid bare on the stage, but here imagination and good theatre-sense have triumphed" in the "skeleton set and selective lighting"; although "such juggling with time can be tiresome," in this case the "frequent dips into the past are so smoothly managed that the main flow of the story towards its tremendous climax is never checked."

Yet even here there is a failure to remark the extent to which the effectiveness of both the set and the time-switching is due to their essential interdependence.

The naturalistic realism of the earlier plays would have been inappropriate. It would have been wrong to bring Willy's Chevrolet on to the stage for a polishing, even if Miller had been inclined to repeat the errors of *The Man Who Had All the Luck*. The car-polishing is recalled from the family past, not something happening in the dramatic present. That this is a play the main action of which is being seen by the audience through the mind of its central character cannot be too often emphasised. The shifts of Willy's consciousness shuttling on a loom of memory demand the maximum fluidity of movement, the minimum of scenery. The alternative of dispensing with scenery altogether had the precedent of *Our Town* to commend it, but Thornton Wilder's evocation of a New England town on the stage with the aid of a few chairs and a loquacious stage-manager had succeeded only because Grover's Corner was Everytown and did not need localising. Willy Loman's house is not as universal, nor is Willy Everyman. As Miller himself once tartly observed "Well, it's obvious that Willy Loman can't be an average American man, at least from one point of view; he kills himself."[9] Spatially the house is individualised as Willy's mortgaged property; temporally it is haunted by the ghosts of his localised past.

To speak of the action containing flashbacks is to miss its point; for "flashbacks" I would prefer to substitute the more cumbersome but more accurate phrase "scenes of recall." Moreover, the sequence in which they are recalled is not chronological, random, or wholly consciously controlled by Willy. I have seen it suggested that the scene with the woman in the hotel bedroom is deferred until the end in order to give momentum and sensation to the flagging action. It has, however, been so patently prepared for in earlier scenes that to only the most naive spectator will it come as any sort of shock. It is deferred to the end by Willy's unconscious, for it is the one piece of the past that he least wishes to recall, the one that he has most successfully repressed. When circumstances have forced him to face it in his conscious mind, the action is truly at an end, for no longer can Willy escape the recognition of his own responsibility for what has happened to his family, no longer

[9]*Tulane Drama Review*, May, 1958, p. 66.

can he conveniently transfer the blame to Howard, to society, to impecuniousness, or even to luck. To argue that in these days of relaxed social morals one minor marital infidelity hardly constitutes grounds for suicide is, paradoxically, to add weight to the theme in the context of this play: for Willy Loman it *is* enough. He has not only, as he sees it, betrayed Linda and Biff, he has betrayed himself. Hap Loman can, with cheerful irresponsibility, seduce the fiancées of executives: the moral code by which Willy wants to live is significantly different from the one in which he has tried to bring up his sons. It is in this sense that Biff can call him a phony or, with greater tolerance, suggest that "He had the wrong dreams. All, all wrong." Coming near to recognising himself at the end, however, Willy can still turn to suicide in the pathetically mistaken belief that it will strengthen his family's gratitude to him.

What I am saying about the play's structure has been said with some authority in the language of another discipline. Within eight months of its opening on Broadway a neuropsychiatrist had published an encomium of it as:

> Visualized psychoanalytic interpretation woven into reality . . . [a] masterful exposition of the unconscious motivations in our lives. It is one of the most concentrated expressions of aggression and pity ever to be put on the stage.[10]

By some of the details of the argument the layman may be unconvinced (the play as "an irrational Oedipal blood-bath," the dinner to which Willy is invited as a totem-feast in which "the sons recognise the father's authority and sexual rights," and Willy's departure to the cloakroom as "castration-panic"), but its emphasis on the importance of the hallucinatory memory-sequences recognises one of the play's original contributions to dramatic structure:

> The past, as in hallucination, comes back to him; not chronologically as in "flash-back," but *dynamically with the inner logic of his erupting volcanic unconscious.* In psychiatry we call this "the return of the repressed," when a mind breaks under the invasion of primitive impulses no longer capable of compromise with reality.

The interweaving of past and present in this play succeeds, of course, because of the organic relevance of the remembered

---

[10]Daniel E. Schneider, "Play of Dreams," *Theatre Arts*, October, 1949, pp. 18–21.

episode to Willy's present situation. However unfamiliar Miller may claim to have been with Freudian psychology, he has certainly developed the motivating "inside-of-his-head" idea so smoothly and unobtrusively as to give the play a dramatic coherence more pleasing and more compulsive than his earlier more conventionally well-made plays had had.

It is, of course, a play about a man and his sons, about what we have since come to call "the generation gap"; Miller, however, is careful not only to avoid moral judgments himself, but also to discourage us from moral judgments by not taking sides and by leaving deliberately vague and unverifiable many aspects of the Loman family's past and present.

Eric Bentley asks:

> Are the sons of Willy *seen* with the eye or just constructed from the *idea* that the present generation is "lost?" Is Uncle Charlie [*sic*] of Alaska more than a sentimental motif? Is Willy's marriage *there* for us to inspect and understand down to its depths?

To each of these questions the answer is that these things are seen subjectively and developed only as far as Willy himself is capable of taking them. Only twice does Miller attempt to provide a brief external commentary, and to have used any character in a role comparable to that of Alfieri in *A View from the Bridge* would falsify the whole play: we must see Willy's story as Willy sees it.

This is not, however, to encourage the reader to identify himself with Willy or with any other character. The author concentrates on the diversity of forces at work and wants his audience to retain the capacity for objective judgment rather than for emotional identification. At the same time it has an expressionistic aspect in its concern with the external world as perceived by the mind of the dreamer; although it does not carry the distortion and fragmentation of that image to the lengths usually associated with expressionism. This mixture of methods does not work out completely successfully in the theatre, for a confusion of response is almost inevitable. That it should have been attempted at all is evidence of a theatrical adventurousness that is itself a sign of health.

Its appeal to the ordinary theatre-goer on both sides of the Atlantic is also a measure of Miller's success, even though some of its admirers may tend to sentimentalise it. Willy himself is a sentimentalist, particularly where the past is concerned, but the sentimentality that is in that respect a necessary element might have been a little more effectively distanced, especially in the "Requiem." The problem here is Linda. With none of the pathetic obsessions of Kate Keller and without the streak of unreasoning malice that Kate exhibits toward Ann, Linda is just too good for Willy and thus too good for the play. I do not mean that Linda is idealised; she is the most decently moral member of the family, but her devotion and loyalty to Willy are slightly over-emphasised and over-articulated. In the "Requiem" it is her emotion more than its cause to which we respond, because she is herself confused about its cause. The Willy for whom she weeps is not worth her tears for what he is, so much as for what he might have been, and although our vicarious experience of sadness is a normal enough response to another's bereavement, in this case it is obscuring for us the perspective that the play should have sustained. Linda's tears are for humanity, Biff is talking about an individual, Happy is striking an attitude, while Charley is extemporising on an idea. All are characteristic reactions to the situation, and their very diversity is in keeping with the sense of multiplicity that the play has established. The difficulty is that an audience, instinctively expecting a summing-up, fastens on the dominant note, which is Linda's grief, and identifies itself with it. The fault is not entirely Miller's, although in a moment of self-criticism he confessed "My weakness is that I can create pathos at will. It is one of the easiest things to do."[11]

It is also in part the outcome of his moral earnestness, for earlier in the play he has used Linda as a mouthpiece with a lack of subtlety that has often been commented on (though sometimes exaggerated). This occurs at a culminating point of Act I, and, being the one scene in that act which does not take place inside Willy's head, gains an added air of objective reality. The whole scene ought to be judged in its context, but one part of one speech insists on isolating itself:

> I don't say he's a great man. Willy Loman never made a lot of money. His name was never in the paper. He's not the finest character that ever lived. But he's a human being, and a terrible thing is happening to him. So attention must be paid. He's not to be allowed to fall into his grave like an old dog. Attention, attention must be finally paid to such a person. (p. 44)

[11]*Theatre Arts*, October 1953, p. 34.

The "attention" that she demands for him is out of proportion to
the situation; it seems to be an attention more penetrating, more
far-reaching, than can reasonably be expected of his sons (from
whom, anyway, she is really demanding sympathetic understanding, not attention). Mary McCarthy comments on "the shrill,
singsong voice of the mother":

> She is really admonishing the audience that Willy is, as she says, "a
> human being." But that is just it; he is a Human Being without
> being anyone, a sort of suffering Statistic. The mother's voice raised
> in the old melancholy Jewish rhythms ("Attention must be paid"
> is not a normal American locution; nor is "finally," placed where it
> is; nor is "such a person" used as she uses it) seems to have been
> summoned from some other play that was about particular people.

The implication that this would have been a better play had
Miller rooted it more firmly in a Jewish milieu makes an attractive
hypothesis, especially in the light of the success of Bernard Kops
and Arnold Wesker in Britain a little later. Miss McCarthy argues
that Willy "could not be Jewish because he had to be American."
Miller had a better reason than this: a markedly Jewish Willy
Loman might have made the play seem an attack on covert anti-
Semitism in American business. By making Willy ethnically
neutral Miller emphasises his point that Willy's trouble is that he is
Willy in a particular society, not that he is a Jew, or a salesman, or a
representative of any other group. In this one speech he is being
presented as, in Miss McCarthy's words:

> A subject for the editorial page, which could take note of his
> working conditions, ask for unemployment benefits and old-age
> care for him, call "attention" in short, to the problems of the
> salesman in the Welfare State.

But Linda's speech throws into too high a relief something which
is only one part—and that not the main—of a play more complex
than it seems.

Of *Our Town* Miller once remarked: "I think that if the play
tested its own theme more remorselessly, the world it creates of a
timeless family and a rhythm of existence beyond the disturbance
of social wracks would not remain unshaken."[12] This more re-

---

[12]"The Family in Modern Drama," *Atlantic*, 197 (April, 1956), 35–41; reprinted in *Modern Drama*, eds. Travis Bogard and William Oliver (New York:
Oxford University Press, 1965).

morseless testing of the theme is what *Death of a Salesman* attempts, and the sentimentality that Linda brings to it really comes from the "timeless family" and the "rhythm of existence" of *Our Town*. Linda is the one character is this play who ought to have been developed more fully because of her importance in the two scenes that do not take place inside Willy's head. As it is, she is too much "The Mother" and not enough an individualised Linda Loman.

Miller's comment on *Our Town* is offered in amplification of this proposition: "Every form, every style, pays its price for its special advantages. The price paid by *Our Town* is psychological characterisation forfeited in the cause of the symbol." The price paid by *Death of a Salesman* might be said to be psychological characterisation misunderstood in the audience's eagerness for a symbol and in their confusion over the form. The Cobb interpretation of Willy would have made him more of an individual, less of the Everyman, but, perhaps because of human sympathy for underdogs, the "little man" image and the victim symbol seem to have predominated.

Perhaps the structure of the play does not make clear early enough the subjective angle from which Willy is being viewed; it begins so much like a realistic play that we have come to accept it as such before the first memory-sequence occurs, and we are not quick enough to see it as "the inside of his head." Yet if we will accept Willy as a character rather than a symbol or an abortive attempt at a tragic hero, some of the play's problems can better be kept in perspective. Even Mary McCarthy is prepared to allow some greatness to her "suffering Statistic" for she, like Philip Hope-Wallace, sees in him analogies with King Lear, but also has some reservations: "Lear, however, has the gift of language, which is not just a class-endowment, for the Fool has it too. This gift of language is what makes him human and not just 'a human being.'" Shakespeare writing *King Lear*, however, is under no obligation to make an ancient Briton or his Fool speak like the seventeenth-century audience watching them. A twentieth-century audience could not be expected thus willingly to suspend its disbelief if a twentieth-century salesman used an idiom so markedly different from its own. Whether the action takes place inside or outside his head, the language must be realistic; whether he is Cobb's "man rejoicing in his enormous vitality" or Muni's "sad little chap beaten from the start," he is confused in his aspirations and certainly no more articulate than are those around him. If in *All My Sons* the characteristic idiom is the unanswered question, in *Death of a Salesman* it is the cliché worn so smooth as to limit communication to the superficial and the unimportant. Poetry in the language would be inappropriate, except to the extent that an occasionally heightened phrase acquires memorability. The poetry is in the characterisation and the theme. When, in the exceptional speech, Linda's idiom is heightened, it is heightened into the public statement. "No one could write an editorial calling attention to the case of King Lear," says Mary McCarthy with justice, but it is this speech with its rhetoric, not the play as a performed whole, that approaches the editorial. Yeats's distinction may be helpful: "We make out of our quarrel with others rhetoric" (which is what Linda's speech does), "but out of our quarrel with ourselves, poetry." Though he does not fully recognise it, Willy is engaged throughout the play in a quarrel with himself, and out of it comes a kind of poetry, muted and non-Shakespearian, but by no means contemptible. Only to the extent that it echoes "the still, sad music of humanity" does it make Willy a symbol of the human condition.

Who Killed the Salesman?

Sighle Kennedy

It was on the night of February 10, 1949, that Willy Loman first rushed off a Broadway stage. As his wife cried out after him in fear, "Willy? Willy, answer me!," the theater was filled with the roar of a car starting and speeding away. Then a crash. And the audience knew that Salesman Willy Loman had wrecked the car and killed himself to leave his family $20,000 insurance money. No one on the stage tried to deny the fact. Willy Loman—the hero of Arthur Miller's play, *Death of a Salesman*—was a suicide.

To the thousand people who filed out of the theater that night, and to the 400,000 people who have seen the play since then in New York City alone, the vision of Willy Loman has been (let the critics speak for the rest) "overpowering," "shattering," "unforgettable." It has made most of them feel, not "there but for the grace of God go I," but, "there go I right now unless the grace of God (or some agnostic substitute) suddenly acts to stop me."

The questions of whether or not *Death of a Salesman* is a great dramatic structure, or whether or not its writing is splendid or only roughly adequate, can hold but secondary importance in any discussion of the play. Above them one fact shines! Willy Loman, egotistical, greedy, affectionate, lonely, has risen up as a modern Everyman.

But the very way in which Willy speaks so immediately to so many people has brought his problems into sharp and varied scrutiny. The play is now being given not only by four companies throughout the U.S. but by groups in England, Switzerland, Italy, France, Austria, Germany, Greece, Argentina, Israel, and by another four groups in Scandinavia. It speaks not only to, and for the problems of, an American audience but to countries whose insecurity is even more obvious than that of the U.S. represented

Sighle Kennedy, "Who Killed the Salesman?" *Catholic World*, 170 (May 1970), 110–116. Reprinted by permission of the publisher.

by Willy—countries which often look toward the U.S. as an easy
and automatic way out of their troubles. To them, as to Americans,
the self-destroyed Willy rises up in warning.

So powerfully projected and personally received has been this
story of Willy Loman that a not-surprising doubt has risen up
about it. People see in it an accurate picture of their own mental
stresses and feel defensive about Willy. Many of them wonder: was
Willy really responsible for his death, or was he, as Luke Carroll in
the *Herald Tribune* put it, "a pathetic little man caught in an
undertow that's much too strong for him?"

Gene Lockhardt, who plays the part of Willy in New York, has
been impressed by the earnest tone of his fan letters and visitors.
"So many of them," he commented when interviewed for this
article, "begin by saying, 'You know, the play made me think.' "

Was Willy the victim of brute economics? or of an unbounded,
irrational desire for success? or of the thoughtless ingratitude of
his sons? These questions and many others have remained with
the *Salesman*'s audience long after the final curtain has gone down.

Perhaps the largest single group that thinks of Willy as a helpless
"little man" is made up of those who see economics as the all-
powerful factor in the play. They make the most of the epitaph
spoken by Willy's friend, Charley: "Nobody dast blame this man.
For a salesman there is no rock bottom to the life. He don't put a
bolt to a nut, he don't tell you the law or give you medicine. . . . A
salesman is got to dream, boy. It comes with the territory." The
territory, they say (and have said all along), is to blame. Willy had
no chance against the capitalistic system.

The other half of the group is at the opposite extreme of belief.
They also feel that economics is the determining power in the play,
but they believe that Miller, in criticizing "the territory," is trying
to undermine democracy. "It's not true that the *Death of a Salesman*
gives a true picture," said one indignant businessman at a Cham-
ber of Commerce Executive's meeting in St. Louis. "The professional salesman has . . . a life built upon the foundation stone of
attitude, knowledge, integrity and industry."

Such a group contends that Miller has stacked the cards against
Willy and used his single tragedy to point an unjustifiable finger at
salesmanship itself. If Willy died, they say in effect, Arthur Miller
killed him.

But most people who saw the play or read it (200,000 copies
have been distributed through the Book-of-the-Month Club alone)

do not feel that either of these exclusively economic views is sufficient to explain Willy's death.

A more percipient businessman speaking through *Fortune* magazine, the very Valhalla of salesmanship, said. "Willy represents any man whose illusions have made him incapable of dealing realistically with everyday life." The article was entitled "A Salesman is Everybody."

If one hears out the play with an open mind, it is hard not to agree with this last opinion. Far from painting a one-sided economic picture, Miller is almost painfully scrupulous in showing that Willy's tragedy must not be set at the door of his particular type of work (symbolic though that surely is). Willy's braggadocio, his confidence that he and his sons, by divine right of personality, are above the laws that bind ordinary men, put his acts in the realm of universal moral censure—not in the cubby-hole of an ideology.

Even more specific proof of the play's lack of bias is the fact that Charley, Willy's neighbor and sincere friend, is a successful businessman. Charley not only lends Willy money, but constantly tries to help him out of his self-pity, to calm the frustrated rages which finally lead him to madness.

When Willy is fired by the ungrateful son of his old boss, Charley offers him a job. Willy, from vanity, will not accept. The only reason that Willy can make his final grand gesture of leaving insurance money is because Charley has been paying the last installments. Grudgingly, Willy says: "Charley, you're the only friend I've got. Isn't that a remarkable thing?" Charley takes no credit for his good neighbor policy, only wryly remarks at one point: "You sneeze in here, and in my house hats blow off."

With Charley living next door, economics can hardly be termed the nemesis of Willy's life. His failure as a man is the cause, rather than the effect, of his economic failure.

But the working of Willy's mind, confronted shockingly as it is with life, death and the terrible insecurities that grow up between the two, has also fascinated psychologists—professional and amateur alike. It is interesting to note that their suggestions, in true detective-story fashion, implicate almost every other member of the cast.

The one character who can be immediately absolved from suspicion is Linda, Willy's wife. In spite of the fact that Willy, with all his bragging, has barely made enough to support his family, and although he treats her with increasing rudeness as his discontent drives him more and more inside himself, her goodness never fails. She loves and explains Willy without ever being able to reach him. Her speeches are touching, but rather harrowing, in their helplessness: "I search and search and I search, and I can't understand," she says, " . . . I live from day to day."

Her one positive action is to cry out for help, and her voice does reach her two careless sons—"Attention," she insists, "attention must be finally paid to such a man. He's a human being and a terrible thing is happening to him. He's not to be allowed to fall into his grave like an old dog."

The sons, Biff and Happy, inherit their father's worst qualities, and the various tensions between them leave plenty of scope for all sorts of analysis. Biff, the older and more gifted in every way, at first seems destined to fulfill all his father's dreams. In school he was handsome, popular, a great athlete, a leader. Willy idolizes his son and fills him with contempt for humdrum responsibilities.

When Biff steals school footballs, Willy laughingly calls it "initiative." When he bullies his classmates and cheats at exams, his father encourages him, thinks him "a fearless character." But when, in a crucial examination, Biff runs up against a professor he can neither bluff nor cheat, he learns that his father has failed him doubly. He follows Willy to Boston to ask for help—and finds him in a hotel with a woman. Suddenly he senses, rather than sees, the complete falsehood of his father's life—and the falsehood of the life he himself has been brought up to lead.

Hopelessly indulged, however, as he is, he has no values now to give him balance. Even Willy's shame and contrition ("She's nothing to me, Biff, I was just lonely, terribly lonely.") merely harden him. At the final action of the play Biff is thirty-four, still unsettled. He is satisfied only when he is working on a farm, but keeps drifting because of a recurrent dread of "not getting anywhere."

Biff's failure is one of the things that Willy will not let himself face. "It's all spite . . . spite," he tries to believe. Linda never knows the reason for the break between father and son but she knows that his sons represent the hardest part of Willy's punishment. "I tell you," she pleads with them, "he put his whole life into you and you've turned your backs on him. . . . Biff, his life is in your hands."

Biff's sympathy for his father's suffering finally does overcome his resentment. He makes a last desperate attempt to open Willy's eyes to the truth—to make him understand that neither of them can achieve the success for which Willy has hoped—"Pop, I'm nothing. . . . Can't you understand that? Will you take that phony dream and burn it before something happens?"

But Willy's warped mind can no longer follow any bent but its own. He only senses the affection in Biff's voice and this knowledge leads ironically to a resurrection of all his flashiest ambitions. "That boy," he cries out pathetically, "that boy is going to be magnificent! Can you imagine that magnificence with twenty thousand dollars in his pocket? When the mail comes he'll be ahead of Bernard again!" (Bernard is Charley's lawyer-son, of whose success Willy cannot help but be jealous.) And Willy rushes off to death for money that nobody wants—money that helps nobody.

Happy, the second son, represents no such dramatic struggle. He is a marked-down version of his father, with not even a grand dream to cover his grossness. His only redeeming aspect is an easy-going fondness for his family.

One psychiatrist (Dr. Daniel Schneider writing in *Theatre Arts*) has interpreted the whole play as a dream of Happy's to get revenge on his father for paying more attention to Biff than to him—resolving the play into death by compound Oedipus complex!

The last important personage—and the most baleful—is a man who has been dead fifteen years. Ben, Willy's older brother, is a symbol of the ruthless success Willy has never reached. "There was the only man I ever met," Willy says, "who knew all the answers." He has treasured up the memory of Ben until it is more real to him than any of the people in his life.

The figure of Ben materializes again and again on the stage and Willy savors his favorite brag: "When I was seventeen I walked into the jungle and when I was twenty-one I walked out. And, by God, I was rich."

"Rich," echoes Willy, thinking of his sons, "that's just the spirit I want to imbue them with! To walk into a jungle!" Willy has absorbed the spirit of Ben's jungle tactics, "Never fight fair with a stranger, boy. You'll never get out of the jungle that way." He comes to think of life, not as a mutually helpful state, but as a jungle, "dark but full of diamonds."

One very significant scene shows the struggle of Willy between two worlds: the destructive dream of Ben and the real world of Charley who is trying to distract him by asking about his work, by playing casino. In spite of all Charley's efforts, Willy's mind keeps slipping back to Ben whom he sees as clearly as he does Charley. He keeps trying to talk to both at once, getting more and more confused.

Suddenly, to cover up his mistakes, Willy accuses Charley of cheating at the cards and sends him home hurt and baffled. The voice of Ben speaks out more and more clearly: "Twenty thousand—that *is* something one can feel with the hand, it is there. . . . It does take a great kind of man to crack the jungle. . . . One must go in to fetch a diamond out." Ben's words and example—grown to an obsession—directly lure Willy to his death.

The very multiplicity of problems which confront Willy must put us on our guard against placing too much stress on any one of them. Yet if no single cause compelled Willy's suicide, was it perhaps the sum of all of them? Two facts seem to answer this last question. This first is the action of the play itself. Miller has shown Willy, through the years, letting his vanity and pretensions undermine his sense of right and wrong. He repays those who try to help him only with contempt. At the end of the play he has swollen to the dreadful traditional figure of tragedy—destroyed by a single cancerous fault.

The second fact (if this first is not sufficient) is the testimony of Miller himself. In several very earnest articles he has made clear his belief that a play based on pathos—"pity for a helpless victim"—presents an essentially false view of life. The contrast to pathos is tragedy, he says, "which must illustrate a principle of life. . . . Our lack of tragedy may be partially accounted for by the turn which modern literature has taken toward the purely psychiatric view of life, or the purely sociological.

"If all our miseries, our indignities are born and bred within our minds, then all action, let alone the heroic action is obviously impossible. And if society alone is responsible for the cramping of our lives, then the protagonist must be so pure and faultless as to force us to deny his validity as a character. From neither of these views can tragedy derive, simple because neither represents a balanced concept of life."

In theory as in dramatic practice, Miller shows the same brave and deliberate effort to meet problems "in head-on collision"— and take the consequences. His stated aims not only show him well worth a thoughtful hearing, but they set a very high standard for judgment of his work. He believes that "tragedy brings not only sadness . . . but knowledge. What sort of knowledge? In the largest sense of the word it is knowledge pertaining to the right way of living in the world . . . Tragedy . . . makes us aware of what the character might have been. But to say . . . what a man might have been requires of the author a soundly based, completely believed vision of man's greatest possibilities."[1]

Does *Death of a Salesman* "make us aware of what Willy Loman might have been"? Another statement of Miller's, this one marking the play's first birthday on Broadway, supplies a clue to the answer. He notes several disappointments—"one above all. I am sorry the self-realization of the older son, Biff, is not a weightier counterbalance of Willy's disaster."

Certainly, Biff, if anyone, should be the one to demonstrate what Willy "might have been" and what the "right way of living" is which might have saved him. What does Biff say? He says—"I'm nothing"—at least the beginning of wisdom. He further implies that his value will consist in doing the outdoor physical work he is best fitted for.

At Willy's grave, he thinks of what his father has thrown away—"There were a lot of nice days. When he'd come from a trip; or on Sundays, making the stoop. . . . You know something, Charley, there's more of him in that front stoop than in all the sales he ever made." Charley agrees: "He was a happy man with a batch of cement."

True and touching as these reminiscences are, they seem on another level entirely from the dreams, the furies ("all, all, wrong") that are shown at work in Willy. These driving forces, which all of us have felt pressing on our lives from one direction or another indeed seem to call for a "weightier counterbalance" than these words of Biff provide.

From the character of Charley, too, we might expect some statement of vision, but Charley never seems able to illumine the principle that underlies his good deeds. This lack appears in terrible relief when, after being fired, the disillusioned Willy says to him: "After all the highways, and the trains, and the

---

[1] Arthur Miller, "The Nature of Tragedy," *The New York Herald Tribune*, March 27, 1949; reprinted in *The Theatre Essays of Arthur Miller*, ed. Robert A. Martin (New York: Viking, 1978), pp. 9–10.

appointments, and the years, you end up worth more dead than alive." Charlie's answer is not only negative, but a double negative. "Willy," he says, "nobody's worth nothing dead." How very little light that sheds on the right way of living!

At Willy's grave Charley shows more insight. When Linda wonders that Willy should choose death when "he only needed a little salary," Charley replies: "No man only needs a little salary." (A reply which manages to strike at the root of all economic materialisms.)

What might Willy Loman have been? What can Biff Loman become? These great possibilities are left for each person in the audience to answer for himself. Brooks Atkinson noted in his review: "Miller has no moral precepts to offer. . . . He is full of pity, but he brings no piety." Taken in the largest sense, as Miller would want it to be, this can only indicate a grave defect in his play's total vision. Even the "self-realization" of Biff turns in-evitably into another question. If no man's satisfaction can be found in a "little salary," can it really rest ultimately in a little "cement"?

In spite of the fact, however, that *Death of a Salesman* ends so, with a question rather than an answer, Arthur Miller has performed in its creation an act of truly heroic stature. His far-reaching, sympathetic and insistent formulation of Willy's question has made millions of Willys in his audience care deeply about the answer—the best way, surely, of spurring them to find it.

Point of View in Arthur Miller's
Death of a Salesman

Brian Parker

In *Death of a Salesman* Arthur Miller wrote far better than he seems to have realized, at least if we may judge by his critical essays on the play.[1] This is true of both the play's content—its analysis of American values—and of its technique. Miller's recent *After the Fall* uses the same nonlogical, subjective memory structure as the earlier play, and uses it far more consistently and skilfully, and yet is far less effective in engaging the self-identification by the audience for which expressionism strives. And this is not only because the experience examined in *After the Fall* is less common than the disaster of Willy Loman, but because the very hesitancies of technique in *Death of a Salesman*, its apparent uncertainty in apportioning realism and expressionism, provide a dramatic excitement of a more complex kind than Miller achieves in his later, more consistent plays.

To claim to understand a play better than its author does may sound egotistic, but we may take comfort from the fact that Miller himself says in the Preface to his *Collected Plays*:

> ... a writer of any worth creates out of his total perception, the vaster proportion of which is subjective and not within his intellectual control. ... if it is art [that the playwright] has created, it must by definition bend itself to his observation rather than to his opinions *or even his hopes*.[2]

It is the contention of this paper, therefore, that by keeping close

---

[1] Preface, *Arthur Miller's Collected Plays* (New York, 1960); "*Death of a Salesman:* a symposium," *Tulane Drama Review*, II (1958); "Tragedy and the Common Man," *Theatre Arts*, XXXV (1951), 48–50.

[2] Preface, *Arthur Miller's Collected Plays*, 36–7; see also 8: ". . . in his conscious intention the artist often conceals from himself an aim which can be quite opposed to his fondest beliefs and desires."

to actual observation *Death of a Salesman* presents a far more accurate weighing of American values than Miller's subsequent analyses suggest, and that the blurred line between realism and expressionism is not the weakness some critics have claimed, but, on the contrary, one of the play's most subtle successes.

The realism in *Death of a Salesman* is fairly obvious, and reflects the influence on Miller of Henrik Ibsen, the Ibsen, that is, of the middle phase, the great realist reformer. In *All My Sons* and *Death of a Salesman* Miller adopts Ibsen's "retrospective" structure, in which an explosive situation in the present is both explained and brought to a crisis by the gradual revelation of something which has happened in the past: in *Death of a Salesman* this is, of course, Willy Loman's adultery, which by alienating his son, Biff, has destroyed the strongest value in Willy's life. This structure is filled out with a detailed evocation of modern, urban, lower-middle class life: Miller documents a world of arch-supports, aspirin, spectacles, subways, time payments, advertising, Chevrolets, faulty refrigerators, life insurance, mortgages, and the adulation of high school football heroes. The language, too, except in a few places which will be considered later, is an accurate record of the groping, half inarticulate, cliché-ridden inadequacy of ordinary American speech. And the deadly realism of the picture is confirmed for us by the way that American audiences have immediately recognized and identified with it in the theatre.

However, even in his realist plays, Ibsen has details which, while still being acceptably probable, have also a deeper, symbolic significance: one thinks of such things as the polluted swimming baths in *The Enemy of the People*, the eponymous wild duck, or, more abstractly, the hair and pistols motifs in *Hedda Gabler*. Such a deepening of realism is also a technique in *Death of a Salesman*. Consider, for instance, the value that Willy and his sons attach to manual work, and its glamorous extension, sport, their belief that it is necessary for a man to keep fit, to be able to handle tools and build things. Willy's handiness around the house is constantly impressed on us: "He was always good with his hands," Linda remembers, and Biff says that his father put more enthusiasm into building the stoop than into all his salesmanship; in his reveries Willy again teaches his boys how to simonize a car the most efficient way, and is contemptuous of his neighbour Charlie, and Charlie's son Bernard, because they lack the manual skills; Willy's favourite son, Biff, is even more dextrous than his father— in high school he was a star athlete and, as a man, he can find happiness only as a ranch hand; one remembers that Willy's father was a pioneer type who drove over the country in a wagon, earning money by ingenious inventions and the making of flutes. Willy's mystique of physical skill is thus a reflection of the simpler, pioneer life he craves, a symptom and a symbol of his revolt against the constraints of the modern city.

Slightly more abstract, yet still realistic, is the play's use of trees to symbolize the rural way of life which modern commercialism is choking. Willy, we are told, bought his house originally because it stood in a wooded suburb where he could hunt a little, and where his yard was flanked by two great elms; but now the trees have been cut down and his property is so over-shadowed by apartment houses that he cannot even grow seed in his back garden. (The choked seed is a fairly obvious symbol: Willy Loman is trapped in a society which prevents him establishing anything to outlast himself, ruining the lives of his sons as well as his own.) We learn at the beginning that it is dreaming about the countryside and watching scenery, particularly trees, which is the main cause of Willy's recent road accidents; it is to look after timber that Willy's brother, Ben, tries to persuade him to go to Alaska; the "jungle," Ben says, is the place for riches; and at moments of crisis Willy yells "The woods are burning," a phrase which is nonsensical unless seen in context of the other tree references.

The last example is already diverging from realism: that is, it is not a phrase habitually used in American life; it needs the context of the play to give it meaning. And when we find Miller directing that, whenever Willy remembers the past, the stage be drenched in a green, checkered pattern of leaves, then it is obvious that the technique has moved from realistic symbolism to outright expressionism.[3]

The set for the play, designed by Jo Mielziner but to Miller's specifications, and influenced, no doubt, by the set for O'Neill's *Desire under the Elms*, is a bizarre but wholly successful mingling of

---

[3]The 1963 production at the Tyrone Guthrie Theatre in Minneapolis suffered because it emphasized the realistic aspects of the play and cut down the expressionistic. There were no apartment silhouettes, for example, nor any manipulation of lighting or music.

realism and non-realism. Its skeletal house shows several rooms simultaneously (like mediaeval staging); the house is sparsely furnished with just enough properties to suggest a sense of place and environment,[4] with the result, as the first stage direction suggests, that "an air of dream clings to the place, a dream rising out of reality"; and the house has in front of it a bare, neutral forestage, used (as in the Elizabethan theatre) to represent any place demanded by the story, with necessary props being carried on and off by the characters themselves. The skeletal framework of the house also gives it a sense of fragility which is intensified by surrounding it with the menacing silhouettes of tall apartment houses, producing an effect of claustrophobia, of rural wood menaced by asphalt jungle.

The set is expressionistically lit to reinforce this impression. The apartment silhouettes are bathed in angry orange; when Willy remembers the past, the house is dappled by the green of vanished trees; when Biff and Hap pick up two women and neglect their father, the directions request a lurid red; and at the end, when Willy insanely tries to plant seed by night, the "blues" of the stage direction simultaneously suggests moonlight and his mood of despair. Music is similarly manipulated: the rural way of life is represented by flute music, telling "of grass and trees and the horizon"; it is heard only by Willy whenever he dreams of the life he should have led or of the early days when his suburb was still in the country. It is associated, of course, with Willy's pioneer father, the flute maker; and in the modern world has degenerated to Willy and Biff's unbusinesslike habit of whistling in elevators, and, at a yet further remove, to the mechanized whistling of Howard and his children as played back on a tape recorder. The tape recorder scene is, in fact, a brilliantly compact piece of symbolism, functioning like the "mirror scene" in some of Shakespeare's plays (or Brecht's *"Grundgestus"*) to epitomize the action of the whole play: not only does it illustrate the mechanization of family life, but Howard's idolizing of his children and bullying of his wife exactly parallel Willy's, showing a resemblance between the two men which undercuts left-wing clichés about employer and worker; and, when Willy knocks it over and cannot stop it, the machine

---

[4]All the properties listed in the original stage direction are used or referred to in the course of the play, except the athletic trophy whose symbolic purpose is obvious anyway.

serves as both cause and illustration of Willy's mental breakdown: he has one of his schizophrenic attacks, and the mechanical voices, so like those of his own home life, are an equivalent to the clamorous subconscious of which he has also lost control. The crucial hotel bedroom scene, in which Biff discovers his father's adultery, is heralded by a shrill trumpet blast, and Willy's final disaster is conveyed by musical shorthand: his decision to commit suicide is accompanied by a prolonged, maddening note, which collapses into a crash of discords, to represent the car crash offstage, and then modulates into a dead march to introduce the requiem scene. Certain characters and situations also have what amount to *leit-motifs*: besides the flute music, we are told there is a "boys' music"; raucous sex music for the scene of Biff's discovery and the barroom scene where Biff and Hap pick up women; and a special music to herald the appearances in Willy's memory of his elder brother, Ben.

The presentation of Ben is an important clue as to exactly how, and why, Miller is using expressionism in *Death of a Salesman*. He is distinctly less "real" than the other characters of the play, stiffer, with a more stilted way of speaking: in the original production, Elia Kazan had the part acted unnaturally, like an automaton. Ben seems less "real" than the others because he is not so much a person as the embodiment of Willy's desire for escape and success: Willy calls him "success incarnate." This is proved by the fact that he does not only appear in memory scenes but is summoned up at the end to "discuss" Willy's plan of suicide; obviously, he here represents a side of Willy's own mind. It is interesting to note, therefore, that the stage directions emphasize that Ben always appears at exactly the moment Willy thinks of him, which is not true of the other characters in the memory scenes. The figure of Ben, then, represents not Ben as he actually was, so much as Ben as his image has been warped in the mind of the rememberer, Willy; and this reveals the peculiar nature of expressionism in *Death of a Salesman*.

Miller is not using expressionistic techniques in the way they are used by the German writers of the 1920's, to dramatize abstract forces in politics or economics or history. He is using the techniques solely as a means of revealing the character of Willy Loman,[5] the values Willy holds and, particularly, the way his mind

[5]See Preface, *Collected Plays*, 39

works. Miller's reason for blending realism and expressionism in *Death of a Salesman* is that this combination reflects the protagonist's actual way of thinking: "I wished to create a form," says Miller, "which . . . would literally be the process of Willy Loman's mind."[6] It is Willy Loman's character, therefore, which is the chief link between the two dramatic modes, and this is possible, of course, because Willy is technically a schizophrenic: overwork, worry and, particularly, repressed guilt have resulted in a mental breakdown in which present and past mingle for him inextricably, where, in Miller's own phrase, time is "exploded."

As Miller points out,[7] this is not a "flashback" technique (the film of *Death of a Salesman* failed precisely because it tried to turn the memory sequences into flashbacks); what it does is to present a past distorted by the rememberer's mind—a subjective, not objective record; and the memories have an extra tension because they occur simultaneously with events in the present, more like a double exposure than a flashback. Note, for instance, how the memory scenes appear gradually, usurping the present bit by bit in the card game with Charlie when Willy is talking to the remembered Ben and the actual Charlie simultaneously, or the gradual emergence of the repressed hotel bedroom scene which is brought to a climax when Biff's and Happy's pick-ups enter in the present. This simultaneous presentation of past and present, dream and reality, gives the play a metaphoric quality, a Cocteau-ish "poetry of the theatre," which (in my opinion) compensates for the so often criticized banality of language. Ambiguity, irony, and tension occur in the action and stage pictures, not in the wording where they might, more conventionally, be expected. It is a metaphor in time.

The form of the play, then, depends on the gradual admission by Willy *to himself* of his own guilt; it differs from the public exposés of Ibsen's form in that Willy's adultery is never openly discussed between him and Biff, and Linda and Hap never learn of it at all: the sole importance is that Willy himself should recognize it. Normal chronology is ignored, therefore: the order of events depends on the way that memories of the past swim up out of Willy's memory because of their emotional association with things happening in the present. For example, Willy's worry about

---

[6]*Ibid.*, 23–4.
[7]*Ibid.*, 26.

having nearly crashed his car in the present brings up memories of happy experiences with cars in the past; as Willy eases his feeling of inferiority to Charlie by mocking Charlie's lack of skill with tools, this conjures up the memory of Ben, Willy's ideal of practical success, and leads with emotional but not chronological logic to reminiscences of their pioneer father. Note, particularly, that certain things always "trigger" this kind of mental relapse in Willy because they are so associated with his guilt: silk stockings, for instance, or the sound of women laughing; and the blurring of mental realities is represented visually by characters stepping across the wall lines of the skeletal setting. Miller says: ". . . the structure of the play was determined by what was needed to draw up [Willy's] memories like a mass of tangled roots without end or beginning." This provides a sense of climax because "if I could make him remember enough he would kill himself."[8]

However, Miller's explanation of his purpose fails to account for an important inconsistency in the use of expressionism. The play does not divide neatly into realistic scenes in the present and expressionistic memory scenes in Willy's mind; some of the expressionistic scenes deal with events in the present when Willy is not even there, and cannot therefore be said to be distorted through his schizophrenia. Consider the scenes downtown in Howard's office or the barroom, before Willy arrives, which are represented nonrealistically on the unlocalized forestage; or, most strikingly, the unrealism of the "Requiem" scene, where characters break the wall lines to come downstage, and the forestage itself represents a graveyard. This cannot be a distortion of Willy's mind because Willy is already dead.

The rationale behind the mingling of realism and expressionism is thus uncertain. The result is intriguing. The extension of expressionism to non-memory scenes means that we see even events which Willy did not experience as though through Willy's eyes, as Willy *might* have experienced them. The play's technique thus forces the audience to become Willy Lomans for the whole duration of the play, to sympathize with his predicament in a way they could not do in real life. It allows them to see more than Willy does, but not to see more than he might have seen; they are expected to criticize Willy, but the technique forces them to criticize him from within, as Willy criticizes and condemns

[8]*Ibid.*, 25.

himself. Miller tells us some interesting facts about the genesis of the play which are relevant here:

> The first image that occurred to me which was to result in *Death of a Salesman* was an enormous face to the height of the proscenium arch which would appear and then open up, and we would see the inside of a man's head. In fact, *The Inside of His Head* was the first title. It was conceived half in laughter, for the inside of his head was a mass of contradictions.[9]

The last sentence is particularly important because it reflects on the values of the play in a way which has not yet been analysed: if we see *all* the play as Willy might have experienced it, even those scenes in which he does not actually appear, then *all* the values of the play, good as well as bad, will be restricted to values which Willy might himself have held. The frame of values will be relative to the potential of a character like Willy's, adjusted to the limits of his imagination. This important "point of view" in the play has been invariably neglected: discussions of *Death of a Salesman* assume that it presents Miller's own values, and Miller's defense of Willy as a tragic hero has done nothing to rectify the error.

Obviously, *Death of a Salesman* is a criticism of the moral and social standards of contemporary America, not merely a record of the particular plight of one man. And, also obviously, it presents Willy as a victim of the deterioration of the "American dream," the belief in untrammelled individualism. The word "dream" is a key word, recurring frequently in the play; and the deterioration of American individualism is traced through the Loman generations in a descending scale, from the Whitman-like exuberance of Willy's father, through Ben, Willy himself, to the empty predatoriness of Happy, who is, he admits, compulsively competitive in sex and business for no reason at all.

The ideal of self-dependence has become the vicious competition of the modern business community, of which Willy, as a salesman, is the lowest common denominator. Miller has explained Willy's surname as standing for "low man on the totem pole," the bottom of the heap; and, interestingly, Willy's ideal, the old salesman in green slippers, is called "Dave *Single*man." The

[9]*Ibid.*, 23.

two names contrast Willy's actual exploitation and the dignified independence to which he aspired.

Willy's philosophy is the personality cult of Dale Carnegie, the "win friends and influence people" theory which exploits human relations for purposes of gain. "Be liked and you will never want," Willy advises his sons; and his famous distinction between being "liked" and being "well liked" seems to rest on whether or not the liking can be exploited for practical ends. Such using of friendliness falsifies it and invokes a law of diminishing returns, as Willy's lonely funeral shows. The attitude also encourages empty dreams, reflected economically in advertising and time-payments; it is essentially parasitic, producing, building, planting nothing; and the logical extension of its unrestrained competition is Biff's downright theft. The psychologists explain theft as a form of love substitute; and it is true that Biff's stealing only becomes obsessive after his disillusion with Willy; but much more important is the fact that in the past Willy not only condoned but tacitly encouraged Biff's stealing of a football and lumber from a building lot. Willy's bluffing advice to Biff: "Remember, start big and you'll end big," is startlingly like the dictum of the late notorious Dr. Stephen Ward: "If you want to succeed, start at the top!"

So far, then, the play presents a rather conventional, if very powerful, expression of left-wing attitudes to capitalism which have been common since the 1930's.[10] However, *Death of a Salesman* cannot be simplified into mere propaganda. The naïve interpretation of Willy Loman's plight as the result of exploitation of workers by capitalists is qualified in the play in several important ways. In the first place, Willy's employer, Howard, is not presented as a conscious monster but as a man very like Willy himself, with the same narrow love for his family, the same love of gadgetry, the same empty friendliness. Handy-dandy, which is the master, which is the man? The resemblance of the two men suggests that the basic error must be sought in human nature, not just in a particular economic system. Secondly, Willy's plight is shown to be at least partly the result of his own character; he fails not only because of the pressure of the competitive system, but also because of his incorrigible inability to tell the truth even to

[10]Clifford Odets' *Awake and Sing* has a somewhat similar situation to *Death of a Salesman*: a grandfather commits suicide so his grandson may use the insurance money to fulfill the immigrant dreams the grandfather failed to achieve.

himself, his emotional, nonlogical mode of thought, which allows him flatly to contradict himself, and of which schizophrenia is merely an intensification: where once he confused reality and wish fulfilment, he now confuses reality and an idealized past. Thirdly, the play balances the failure of Willy and his children with the success of Charlie and his son, Bernard, who thrive in the very same system: Charlie and his son do not cheat, they merely work hard; they prosper yet remain kindly, unpretentious, sensitive, helpful. Their presence in the play destroys any interpretation of *Death of a Salesman* as left-wing propaganda. In fact, the exaggerated nature of Bernard's success suggests that Miller partially shares the "American dream" himself; and he has been accused of making a merely vulgar distinction between successful materialism in Charlie and Bernard and unsuccessful in Willy.

However, no consideration of the positive values in *Death of a Salesman* is fair unless it takes into account the play's peculiar point of view. This is the area where the distinction between Miller's observation and the limitations of the Loman sensibility through which the whole play is strained becomes most delicate to trace. The positive values suggested in the play are only such as Willy himself might have arrived at; and it is my purpose to suggest that, deliberately or not, Miller presents them as necessarily limited ideals.

The futile philosophy of Willy Loman is opposed by three main alternatives in *Death of a Salesman*: the pioneering adventurousness of Ben, the sensible practicality of Charlie, and the loyalty of Linda—to list them in order of progressive importance. The values represented by Ben need not detain us very long. Their inadequacy is apparent. Miller's work, as a whole, does reflect a certain admiration for the pioneer virtues of courage and self-reliance, but this is matched by an awareness that such attitudes are dangerous in modern society: the aggressiveness which is admirable in combatting raw nature becomes immoral when turned against one's fellow men. It is the latter, critical attitude which predominates in Miller's picture of Ben, who advises Biff: "Never fight fair with a stranger, boy. You'll never get out of the jungle that way." Clearly, if Willy had gone with Ben to Alaska, he might have been a richer, but he would not have been a better man.

The values represented by Charlie are more important. Charlie is presented as an almost completely sympathetic figure, but Miller includes a few details which prevent any acceptance of Charlie's career as ideal. In the first place, it is suggested, by Charlie himself, that he has had to pay a certain price for his business success, the price of not caring: "My salvation is that I never took an interest in anything." In human terms, Willy's ideal of business, represented by old Dave Singleman, though it is disastrously inaccurate, is more generous than Charlie's calm assurance that "The only thing you got in this world is what you can sell"; it is not without significance that, whereas Willy's idols are the millionaire inventors Edison and Goodrich (one remembers that Willy's father was an inventor), Charlie's is the buccaneer financier, J. P. Morgan. This difference in human warmth between Willy and Charlie comes out in Charlie's tight-lipped reticence, remarked on by Willy as a contrast to his own inability to refrain from chatter. However, the conclusive rebuttal of Charlie's acceptance of the business world comes in the "Requiem": his defence of Willy in the "Nobody dast blame this man" speech, which romanticizes the salesman whose job requires him to dream great things, is immediately rejected by Biff, who maintains that Willy was to blame because he lacked self knowledge, because his dreams were all the wrong dreams, because he let himself be caught in an inhuman system. For all his sympathetic qualities, therefore, Charlie's position is shown to be a compromise: he has succeeded by fitting his character into the existing system, meeting business on its own cold terms. But Biff argues that such a system is too small for a man as imaginative and emotional as Willy. The implication of the "Requiem" is not that Willy ought to have behaved like Charlie, but that he should not have been in business at all.

The most powerful positive value in the play is the value of family loyalty. There is no doubt of Willy's love for his family, particularly for his son, Biff. It is the betrayal of this loyalty which ruins Willy's life, rather than commercial failure, and it is in the name of family love that he finally kills himself, dying "as a father, not as a salesman."[11] But, perhaps because he romanticizes his own father, whom he never knew, Willy has a false ideal of

[11]John Gassner, introduction to *Death of a Salesman* in *Treasury of the Theatre* (New York, 1961), II, 1061.

fatherhood, exposed most blatantly at the very moment when he decides to sacrifice himself for Biff: "Ben, he'll worship me for it." Parental love which is really a disguised form of egotism is a recurrent theme in Miller's work, and the explanation he finds for it is revealed in Willy's reply when Charlie tells him to forget about Biff: "Then what have I got to remember?" As the captain in Strindberg's *The Father* says, children are a materialist's only hope of immortality. But this puts an unfair pressure on the children which perverts a true family relationship.

It is not just Willy's egotism which qualifies the family love in *Death of a Salesman*, however, it is also the fact that it is used as an excuse to ignore other, wider loyalties. And this surely is the great limitation of Linda.

Linda is the most sympathetic character in the play. Her famous "attention, attention must be paid" speech is terribly moving in the theatre, perhaps too moving: Miller has said that his great temptation as an artist is that he finds it too easy to write pathos. And Linda is so sympathetic not only because she is the loyal, downtrodden wife, but also because her attitude seems to sum up many traditional American values. In this connection, I believe no one has yet remarked on the resemblances between *Death of a Salesman* and Robert Frost's poem *The Death of the Hired Man*.[12] Quite apart from the echo in their titles, the situations of the two pieces are strikingly similar: in the Frost poem, the hired man, old Silas, has come "home" ("Something you somehow don't have to deserve") to die; like Willy he is worn out:

> And nothing to look backward to with pride
> And nothing to look forward to with hope.

His employer, Warren, seems at first like Howard in the play, unwilling to keep Silas on because he is too old and unreliable; but Warren's wife, Mary, urges pity in lines which are close to Linda's in both their sentiments and their cadence:

> He never did a thing so very bad
> He don't know why he isn't quite as good
> As anyone. He won't be made ashamed
> To please his brother, worthless though he is.

[12]This resemblance was first pointed out to me by my friend and colleague F. T. Flahiff. Mr. Flahiff, however, does not value the play as highly as I do. Frost's poem was published in 1914 in *North of Boston*.

and she says they must befriend him as they once looked after

> ... the hound that came a stranger to us
> Out of the woods, worn out upon the trail,

recalling Linda's plea that Willy not be allowed to die like an old dog. Mary is also like Linda in her insistence on maintaining the old man's self-respect; Silas' promises to ditch the meadow and clear the top pasture for Warren are like Willy's boasts of future prosperity, face-savers which neither he nor the others really believe; and Willy's inability to accept help from Charlie as a matter of pride is paralleled by Silas' refusal to appeal to his rich brother who is a neighbouring bank director. Like Willy, old Silas is so exhausted that he rambles in his mind, mixing past and present like a dream: "those days trouble Silas like a dream." In particular, Silas harks back to arguments he had with a young college boy who helped with the haying four years before. They argued about how necessary education is to a man, and Silas feels he got the worst of the argument; he wishes he could at least have taught the boy the practical skill of building a load of hay. The feeling here is a mixture of Willy's attitude to Biff and his re-luctant admiration for Bernard. There are several other details where the poem has similar sentiments to the play but in slightly different arrangements: the openings are very similar, in each case an unexpected return, a request for kindness by the loving woman, and the man's affection overlaid by indignation at having been abandoned in the first place, irritably denying his real feeling of responsibility; there is the same Christian-name intimacy, firmly establishing the domestic scale of both play and poem— though the nicknames and diminutives of the play serve the further purpose of conveying the immaturity of Willy's world, on a par with his use of schoolboy slang and the characters telling each other to "grow up"; finally, the most tenuous resemblance is the way that the values represented by the women are associated in both play and poem with the values of unspoiled nature, though this is overt in the poem, implicit in the play. The similarity of the two works, particularly their titles, suggests that Miller was directly influenced by Frost; but even if this is not so, the analogy is still useful in that it highlights the traditional, rural, humane values which Frost hymned his whole career and which the society of *Death of a Salesman* denies. The "hired man" is cared for and pitied; the "salesman" is pitilessly discarded.

Her appeal to these traditional values and her downtrodden, loving loyalty are, however, apt to blind audiences to the essential stupidity of Linda's behaviour. Surely it is both stupid and immoral to encourage the man you love in self-deceit and lies. We are told in the stage directions that Linda has the same values as Willy but that she lacks his energy in pursuing them: it was she who persuaded him not to risk Alaska. Linda does not really believe in his dreams—at least not at the point where we meet her, whatever she may have done earlier; but, without any higher ideals than Willy, she humours him to keep things going. The easygoing negativeness of Hap is the same moral sloppiness pushed one degree farther (Biff is his father's son, Hap is his mother's). After thirty-five years of marriage, Linda is apparently completely unable to comprehend her husband: her speech at the graveside (I don't understand; the house is paid for) is not only pathetic, it is also an explanation of the loneliness of Willy Loman which threw him into other women's arms.

Interestingly, the basic falsity in Linda reveals itself in the rhetoric of her "attention, attention must be paid" speech, with its epizeuxis, inversions, and unnatural cadences. And there is a similar falsity of tone in the other much criticized speech of the play, Charlie's "Nobody dast blame this man. . . ." Whether Miller intended it or not, the falsity of both Linda's loyalty and Charlie's acceptance of business is revealed in the strained language of their rhapsodies. And a more extreme example of the same false rhetoric, very suggestive when we remember that Ben is always distorted to suit Willy's mind, is the notorious: "When I was seventeen I walked into the jungle, and when I was twenty-one I walked out. And by God I was rich." The falsity of these passages, standing out awkwardly from the drabness of speech elsewhere in the play, is, I would suggest, totally appropriate. The values represented by Ben, Charlie, and Linda, though they are more positive than Willy's Dale Carnegie-ism, are in no sense ideal. They are merely values which Willy could have imagined,[13] in rhetoric Willy would applaud (as I have heard Linda's speech applauded in the theatre).

[13]Perhaps this is what Miller is driving at when he says Linda is "made by [Willy] though he did not know it or believe in it or receive it into himself." Preface, *Collected Plays*, 30.

Death of a Salesman, in fact, offers almost no sure values. Arthur Miller appears to recognize this when he says it is a contribution to the "steady year-by-year documentation of the frustration of man," and he moves to a more positive position in his next play, *The Crucible*. But even in *Death of a Salesman* there is one positive gain: Biff at least comes out of the experience with enhanced self-knowledge: "I know who I am, kid." It is not a proud knowledge, rather an admission of limitation and weakness: Biff admits he will never be a big success in the eyes of the world. But such an admission is the beginning of truth; in religious terms it would be called humility (the Preface to *Collected Plays* and *After the Fall* confirm that Miller's interests are finally religious). Moreover, this humility gained by Biff is related to the sacrifice made by Willy. It has been objected, and admitted by Miller, that Willy's stature as a tragic hero is questionable because he dies still self-deceived. But the new truth is there in Biff, and the extension of expressionistic technique beyond Willy's death unbroken into the "Requiem" binds together the two experiences. The extension of the point of view into scenes where Willy does not appear enables the audience at the end to associate Biff's acceptance with Willy's disaster as a single, coherent, and, I would argue, tragic experience; though the technique is closer to *Everyman* than to *Oedipus Rex*,[14] and the audience's identification with the hero's fate is secured by empathy—emotional manipulation of stage techniques—rather than the more usual method of moral sympathy and admiration.

[14]The play's technique of presenting all events and characters as though strained through Willy's mind resembles the Morality technique in which characters and events are all allegories of the central character's psychomachia.

The Right Dream in Miller's
Death of a Salesman

Stephen A. Lawrence

There is no need to point out the contradictions of Miller's *Death of a Salesman*. Enough people have talked about the problems inherent in Charlie's about-face eulogy to Willy and the schizophrenic vacillation of Miller with regard to the problem of responsibility in the play. If Willy is responsible for his own downfall, what are we to make of all the suggestions of a sick and distorted society? And more important, why need we pay any attention to a man so deluded and so unwilling to face up to his limitations that he destroys the potential of his family? If, on the other hand, society is responsible for planting the seeds of corruption and misplaced values in Willy, what are we to make of the success of people like Charlie and his son Bernard who are not only sensible enough to see what is wrong with the American success myth, but apparently strong enough to fly in the face of it and succeed despite it? If Biff was happy out West and Willy is aware enough that he likes working with his hands, why does the Loman family remain where it is, crushed and stifled by surrounding apartment buildings, frustrated by any attempt to implant itself in an environment where nothing can grow?

While few can read *Death of a Salesman* without becoming aware of these contradictions and vagueries, it is worth noting that so many find themselves genuinely moved by the play, and so convinced that the emotion Miller has been able to generate is something more than cheap sentimentality or melodramatic pettiness that they feel the need to somehow defend the play against

Stephen A. Lawrence, "The Right Dream in Miller's *Death of a Salesman*," *College English* 25 (October–May, 1963–1964), 547–49. Reprinted by permission of the publisher.

the harsh criticisms that have been leveled at it. Perhaps there is a way out of the dilemma.

One of the few things that most readers have agreed upon is the characterization of the younger son, Happy. We are aware at the close of the play that Happy is as deluded as ever about his father's worth, even though Biff has reached the point of self-awareness. When Biff, at the funeral, says that his father "had the wrong dreams" and "never knew who he was," we are all relieved to see that perhaps someone can be salvaged from the wreckage. When Happy declares that he is going to take over where his father left off, we share with Biff what Miller refers to as "a hopeless glance at Happy."

Perhaps, though, we have been too quick with our condemnation of Happy. There may be something meaningful and true in his last words which, along with Charlie's eulogy, somehow redeem Willy without contradicting all the clues we have been given to the effect that Willy has caused his own failure. Perhaps there *is* a sense in which both society and Willy are responsible for the death of a salesman, but not in the sense of providing an embarrassing contradiction but a meaningful ambiguity.

Perhaps what is wrong with the society is not that it has implanted the wrong values in him, values which finally do not lead to success anyway, but that it has lost touch with values which should never be relegated only to the personal sphere or the family unit. The apartment buildings closing in on Willy are not closing in only on his house or his family. They represent the crushing of freedom, of individuality, of personality, and most of all, of love. Willy's problem is that he is human enough to think that the same things that matter in the family—especially his love for his son—matter everywhere including the world of social success.

Can we possibly delude ourselves into believing that we like those in the play who represent success? It is curious that of the five of them, only one is represented as having any kind of family life. Howard answers Willy's pleas for human sympathy and consideration with a monstrous dictaphone recording of his son reciting alphabetically the names of the capitals of the forty-eight states. He is obviously more impressed with the machine than he is with his son. Miller has very little time for Dave Singleman, but despite Willy's admiration for this great old salesman, Miller is able to express partly through the man's name the image of a man dying alone in a plush railroad car. Ben, in order to make his fortune, cut his family ties; and in the flashback scene, he shows no human feeling. His speeches too sound more like recorded announcements than the words of a living, feeling person. And it is strange that Charlie is portrayed without a wife, no mention ever being made of the woman who is Bernard's mother. Furthermore the relationship between Charlie and Bernard contrasts with Willy's relationship with Biff by reason of the intense love and hate Willy and Biff have for each other. We never see any emotion between Charlie and his son. In fact when Willy asks Charlie how Bernard was able to become a success when Charlie never showed any interest in him, Charlie makes the curious reply: "My salvation is that I never took any interest in anything." Can this ever be the source of a man's salvation? Perhaps Miller is undercutting the other evidences of kindness in Charlie.

On the other hand we admire Biff for the worship he elicits from his high school friends, even from Bernard. We do not condemn him for the desire to whistle in a public elevator because mature businessmen do not whistle. We do not condemn him for his love of the freedom he found in the West or for his love of his father—a love so strong that his seeing it perverted in the Boston hotel not only breaks his heart but destroys his ambitions. Perhaps what is wrong with Biff is that he has tried to escape to where the problems of love and freedom and individuality do not exist. In this sense we must acknowledge the truth of Happy's closing statement. Yes, Happy is still deluded in thinking that the only important dream is to come out number one man. But this is not all he says. His last words are: "He [Willy] fought it out here, and this is where I'm gonna win it for him." The battle must be fought on the enemy's grounds. Man does not solve his problems as a social animal by retreating out of the society.

This is just why Willy, who is so acutely aware of what it is that makes him happy—opening the windshield and looking up at the sky, building a porch with his own hands, planting seeds in a garden, working in the outdoors—remains to fight in a world which allows a man to succeed only to the extent that he give up what makes him most himself: his freedom, his personality (that which makes him more than just "a dime a dozen"), his belief that there is something worthwhile about being well liked, his love for his son which finally he feels he can prove only at the cost of his life. For it is his lapse from love, his cheap affair with the woman in Boston which destroys the ambition in Biff.

Even at the point when Willy is ready to give up his life, he maintains his belief that somehow there can be a link between love and success. When Biff finally confronts him with the truth of their failure and breaks down crying, Willy is at his peak: "He cried! Cried to me. That boy—that boy is going to be magnificent." Willy may be deluded but his only delusion is that he thinks men can be magnificent because they love. This is not the error of a petty man. Willy *is* a dreamer. But part of the dream is good. Perhaps it is not the part that Happy completely understands. Perhaps the dream is not all wrong, as Biff believes. What redeems Willy is not even the idea of dreaming itself. Charlie is no closer to the truth when he says: "A salesman is got to dream." We are not to settle for the idea that the very fact of dreaming makes men noble. In the Requiem, Happy, Biff, and Charlie all try to grasp at the essence of Willy, but each of them falls short.

Attention must be paid to Willy Loman because he believes in love, which is only the extreme form of being well liked. Willy is destroyed to the extent that both he and the society fail to acknowledge its demands.

The Lost Past in *Death of a Salesman*

Barclay W. Bates

Death of a Salesman has been correctly characterized as a play about the triumph of substance over image, Willy Loman is destroyed because he fails to see that men buy appearances only in their leisure. But *Death of a Salesman* is also about the triumph of the present over the past, Public Willy is the modern gladhanded salesman, but private Willy is four anachronisms: he is the archetypal cherisher of the pastoral world, the pre-industrial-revolution artisan, the ham-handed outlaw frontiersman, and the dutiful patriarchal male intent upon transmitting complex legacies from his forbears to his progeny. Hence one may argue that in a sense it is Willy's civilization, which cannot encourage or even tolerate these anachronisms, that truly destroys him.

The term "pastoral" will be used in this paper in the very broad sense: "The essence of the pastoral is simplicity of thought and action in a rustic setting."[1] In *Death of a Salesman* "pastoral" simplicity is at times the simplicity of the shepherd or hermit, at others that of the farmer, rancher, or frontiersman; however, all the Lomans' dreams of fulfillment in the countryside, plains, or wilderness have a common denominator: the promise of release from the complexity of urban life and obligation, the tangle of the American present.

"A melody . . . played upon a flute,"[2] one of several keynoting images present as the opening curtain rises, is a multivalent symbol, suggestive not only of the past but also of the lost pastoral life. Strongly associated with Willy's wanderer father, it is later

Barclay W. Bates, "The Lost Past in *Death of a Salesman*," *Modern Drama,* 11 (1968–69), 164–72. Reprinted by permission of the publisher.

[1]*The Oxford Companion to English Literature*, ed. Sir Paul Harvey (London, 1962), p. 596.

[2]Arthur Miller, *Death of a Salesman* (New York: Compass Books Edition, The Viking Press, Inc., 1965), p. 11. Subsequent references are to this edition.

often heard as Willy begins his schizoid voyages into bygone years. Similar melodies announce Willy's brother Ben and accompany Ben's brief tale of his and Willy's father. "Small and fine," the melody is equated with the Lomans' "small, fragile-seeming house. Surrounded on all sides by "a solid vault of apartment houses," the anachronistic dwelling, like Willy himself, is diminished and constrained by its environment. These apartment houses of course symbolize urban civilization. Before the set is fully lighted, they are apprehended simply as "towering, angular shapes," reminding one of geometry, the draftsman's board, all the mathematical and technological underpinnings of our modern order. Since the set is "wholly or . . . partially transparent," we see the buildings both above and beneath the one-dimensional roof line of the house, and we are therefore constantly aware of the influence of this civilization upon the tormented occupants of the house.

The action begins as Willy returns from an abortive selling trip to New England. Because the pastoral scenery through which he drove drew him again and again into dreams of the past, he had been unable to drive his car safely: ". . . it's so beautiful up there, Linda, the trees are so thick and the sun is so warm. I opened the windshield and just let the warm air bathe over me. And then all of a sudden I'm goin' off the road!" Willy's inability to control this essential modern machine is a symbolic failure. Committed to the life of the urban and mobile businessman, he cannot succeed in that life. Profoundly attracted by this rustic setting, he must pass hurriedly through it on his errands of commerce. His dramatically central ambivalence is repeatedly and ironically revealed in this opening scene. Pained by Biff's *anomie*, he complains to Linda: "How can he find himself on a farm? Is that a life? A farmhand?" Moments later Willy is angry because the amenities no farmer lacks have disappeared from Brooklyn: "The street is lined with cars. There's not a breath of fresh air in the neighborhood. The grass don't grow anymore, you can't raise a carrot in the backyard. They should've had a law against apartment houses." Willy believes that if Biff got a job selling he "could be big in no time." Yet he fails to see that "big" men and enterprises are responsible for the encroachments he resents. An apostle of free enterprise, he complains about competition: "There's more people! That's what ruining this country! Population is getting out of control. The competition is maddening!"

Willy later appears by himself in the kitchen as *"[t]he apartment houses are fading out, and the entire house and its surroundings become covered with leaves. Music insinuates itself as the leaves appear."* A suggestion of Linda's has transported him in memory to a day in the boys' lost youth. The house is now surrounded by trees and open space. Biff and Happy are polishing Willy's car, which, like the society it symbolizes, looks grand but proves unsatisfactory. Willy discusses with Biff the necessity of pruning a tree, and one is struck by the irony of Willy's complicity in the destruction of things in nature. Willy's reverie is shortly tainted by the appearance of the woman in the Boston hotel room and by signs of Biff's incipient corruption. The mature Happy comes downstairs and gently draws Willy back into the present, but as they talk Willy is reminded of his brother Ben. During the card game with Charley that follows, Willy's mind returns to the day of Ben's first visit to the Loman home.

This first visit is chiefly important for what Ben tells Willy about their mutual father: "Father was a very great and a very wild-hearted man. We would start in Boston, . . . and then he'd drive the team right across the country; . . . And we'd stop in the towns and sell the flutes that he'd made along the way." It is significant that Willy's father began in the entrapping city where Willy, in several senses, ends. Boston is the scene of Biff's catastrophic discovery of Willy and "Miss Francis" in the hotel room. It is also the scene of Willy's claimed sales success (". . . slaughtered 'em in Boston." ". . . go to Slattery's, Boston. Call out the name Willy Loman and see what happens! Big shot!") and the scene of his actual failure. ("The trouble was that three of the stores were half closed for inventory in Boston. Otherwise I woulda broke records.")

As Act II begins, Willy feels that he can talk his boss, Howard, into giving him a New York job and that Biff will secure Bill Oliver's backing in a business venture. About to leave for the office, Willy allows himself to hope that he will once again be able to grow vegetables in his yard. It is obviously no accident that Willy's renewal of interest in planting coincides with his renewal of hope in Biff. Willy's hopes are vain, however, for Biff cannot grow in New York. Before he can mature and be himself fruitful, Biff must reject the success ethic imbued in him by his father and return to the farm. That the formerly "anemic" Bernard begets children before Biff is additional evidence that Willy's teachings are sterile.

During his futile interview with Howard, Willy tells the story of Dave Singleman, the old drummer whose example led Willy to become a salesman. What chiefly inspired Willy was that " . . . old Dave, he'd go up to his room, y'understand, put on his green velvet slippers—I'll never forget—and pick up the phone and call the buyers, and without ever leaving his room, at the age of eighty-four, he made his living." Dave Singleman is hence the ultimate indoorsman; he dies, Willy tells us, "the death of a salesman, in his green velvet slippers in the smoker of the New York, New Haven and Hartford, going into Boston." Slippers become a minor symbol of domestication. Willy wears them as he wanders about outside his house in Act I, and Linda observes that they are incongruous in the outdoors.

Ironically, when Willy finishes his story of Dave Singleman, Howard fires him and leaves him alone in the office. Seemingly at last aware that Singleman's way was the wrong one, Willy is immediately enfolded in the taunting memory of an alternative once offered him by Ben. On his second visit to the Lomans, Ben urges Willy to leave the city and work for him in Alaska. Willy is tempted: "God, timberland! Me and my boys in those grand outdoors!" An outdoorsman in the tradition of the conquistadors, Ben has plunged into the wilderness and torn a fortune from it. Earlier in the play, in an effort to show Ben that he has not lost touch with the old ways, Willy says, "Oh, sure, there's snakes and rabbits and—that's why I moved out here," but Ben never hides his contempt for Willy's tame life.

After the restaurant scene in which Biff admits his own failure, the by then nearly insensate Willy, accompanied by the flute melody, sets off in search of a store where he can buy seeds. Shortly before his final confrontation of Biff at home, Willy is kneeling in his back yard trying to plant the seeds he has purchased. When that last confrontation is over, Willy, at last aware of Biff's steadfast love, forgets his hopes of pastoral fulfillment and sacrifices himself in a vain effort to provide Biff with insurance money to launch a business career. Just before the final curtain falls, the "*hard towers of the apartment buildings rise into sharp focus,*" affirming that the complex urban present has once and for all vanquished Willy Loman.

Like their father, both Biff and Happy are drawn to the out-doors. During the first conversation, Biff tells Happy of the satisfactions of farm life and tries to persuade Happy to return to the West with him. Happy is tempted, but he objects, "The only thing is—what can you make out there?" Like Willy, Happy unreasonably wants both money and the simplicity of a pastoral life. Later in the play Happy tells Willy and Biff of a sporting goods business scheme that would allow Biff and him to live carelessly as they had when they were boys: "And the beauty of it is, Biff, it wouldn't be like business. We'd be out playin' ball again." The idea occurred to Happy while he was in Florida, and both he and his father refer to it as the "Florida idea." Both Willy and Happy have vacationed in Florida; for them it is a pastoral place. Yet it is associated with financial success.

All the Lomans, even Linda, are enthusiastic about the "Florida idea"; their discussion of it is a communion in illusion. Biff is less strongly bound by the success dream than Happy, however, and he is clearly less at home in the city. In his first appearance on stage, he is disturbed by Happy's cigarette smoke—"I can never sleep when I smell it"—just as Willy is earlier disturbed by the odors from neighboring apartment buildings. (One inevitably recalls Dave Singleman's death in the smoker of the New York, New Haven, and Hartford.) In Biff's view urban business en-deavor is "a measly manner of existence" endured "for the sake of a two-week vacation." Biff loves the farm and his praise of farm life and work is lyrical: ". . . it's spring there now, see? And they've got about fifteen new colts. There's nothing more inspiring or beau-tiful than the sight of a mare and a new colt."

Having experienced a meaningful pastoral life, Biff is eventually able to break the bondage created by his father's dreams. As he runs from Bill Oliver's office, he reaches a liberating insight: "I saw the things that I love in the world. The work and the food and the time to sit and smoke . . . all I want is out there, waiting for me the minute I say I know who I am." Hence Biff embraces one part of his heritage and rejects another; choosing the pastoral life, he denies those social forces which lure American men into the marathon pursuit of wealth. He becomes a more conscious and a more human man.

In another time, Willy Loman might have been a happy car-penter. He can put up a ceiling which his brother-in-law, Charley, lauds as a "piece of work." Dreaming of a rustic retirement, Willy hopes to build guest houses on his yearned-for country land for Biff and Happy: " 'Cause I got so many fine tools, all I'd need would be a little lumber and some peace of mind." On the morning of the day which ends with his suicide, he admires his own house: "All the cement, the lumber, the reconstruction I put in this house! There ain't a crack to be found in it anymore." Belittling Charley, Willy says, "A man who can't handle tools is not a man."

But it is important to note that carpentry is no more his work in the world than it is Charley's. Willy marches in Marx's army of alienated labor, performing work that is "not personal to him, is not part of his nature; therefore he does not fulfill himself in work, but actually denies himself. . . . It satisfies no spontaneous urge, but is only a means for the satisfaction of wants that have nothing to do with work."[3] Willy's alienation, however, is perhaps more excruciating than any Marx could have imagined. Business civilization tells Willy that selling is a task as whole and complex as that of any artisan, but the products of Willy's labor are never concrete and observable. The cabinet maker can contemplate the finished cabinet; even the brutalized assembly line worker daily sees a thousand small results of his labor. But Willy can never know the real value of his salesman's skills because many factors—his customers' unique needs and his merchandise's quality among them—contribute to his success or failure. The immediate financial rewards of Willy's work are barely sufficient to provide his family with the necessities and scant comforts of lower middle class life, and the final rewards he anticipates, wealth and eminence, are never in sight. Developing one of the several telling "construction" metaphors, Willy and his brother debate the promise of a salesman's career. Willy insists he is "building something with this firm." Ben replies, "What are you building? Lay your hand on it. Where is it?"

At his death Willy is broke and unemployed. His house is the whole of his estate and the major material achievement of his life. Willy wishes that "Biff would take his house, and raise a family . . . ," but ironically Biff cannot take it because it is built upon the alien ground of the city. Biff is left with only memories, and foremost among them are those of "a lot of nice days. When he'd

[3]Karl Marx, "Alienated Labor," trans. by Eric and Mary Josephson in *Man Alone* (New York, 1962), p. 97.

come home from a trip; or on Sundays, making the stoop; finishing the cellar; putting on the new porch; when he built the extra bathroom." And at last it is Biff who from the heights of redemption and new knowledge can make the definitive comment on his father: "He never knew who he was."

It is worth nothing that although Biff rejects the pettiness and drudgery of a business career, he emulates neither his grandfather, the bearded, wandering flute-maker, nor his uncle, the piratical adventurer. Plainly he lacks his grandfather's craftsman's skills and his uncle's aggressiveness and brutality, but it would be a mistake to conclude that his choice of the farmer's vocation is dictated entirely by his awareness of his limitations and by his basic humanity. Biff also loves the real work of the farmer, just as both he and his father love the real work of the carpenter. Moreover, Biff, like Marx, believes that work should be self-expression. "Men built like we are," he tells Happy at one point, "should be working out in the open."

Just as Willy the outdoorsman and Willy the artisan have no place in urban civilization, neither has Willy the fighter. When a fellow salesman called him a "walrus," Willy "cracked him right across the face." To Charley's mockery of his enthusiasm about Biff's Ebbets Field game, Willy responds with a challenge to fight. Later in the play, when the exasperated Charley asks, "When the hell are you going to grow up?" Willy again challenges him. But violence in this modern order of policemen and law courts is futile and compromising, and Willy, committed to a career of cajolery and manipulation, must perhaps suppress his rage even more than most of his urban brethren.

Hence that rage often finds expression in Willy's diction and in his dealings with his family. His claims and promises of success are expressed in violent figures: "Knocked 'em cold in Providence, slaughtered 'em in Boston," "Oh, I'll knock 'em dead next week. I'll go to Hartford"; "I'm gonna knock Howard for a loop, kid!"; "Knock him dead, boy"; "The world is an oyster, but you don't crack it open on a mattress!" Though Willy never harms Linda, he often yells at her. When the first symptoms of Biff's moral illness appear, Willy sees violence as the proper remedy: "I'll whip him!"

Biff and Happy, however, are more often the instruments of his rage than its objects. Though Willy must earn his living with smiles and talk, he educates his boys in violence. He returns from a selling trip with a punching bag for them, looks on benignly as young Happy manhandles Bernard, and encourages Biff to spar with Uncle Ben. In the play's closing moments, lost in recollection of the day of Biff's Ebbets Field game, he says, "Now when you kick off, Boy, I want a seventy-yard boot, and get down the field under the ball, and when you hit, hit hard. . . ." As the family considers Happy's "Florida idea," Willy cries, "Lick the world! You guys together could absolutely lick the civilized world." Indeed, the Lomans would like to do precisely that.

So taught, Willy's boys are inevitably violent. Adolescent Happy enjoys manhandling Bernard, his intellectual superior. Adult Happy, largely unsuccessful in business, says, "Sometimes I want to just rip my clothes off in the middle of the store and outbox that Goddam merchandise manager." His sexual conquests he describes in metaphors of violence: "I just keep knockin' them over and it doesn't mean anything." Adolescent Biff is "rough with the girls." After he discovers Willy in the Boston hotel room with "Miss Francis," he returns home and senselessly battles Bernard with fists in the Lomans' basement. Adult Biff hopes to "knock [Bill Oliver] for a —." Biff later tells us that when Oliver walked away from him in the office, he "got so mad [he] could've torn the walls down."

Ultimately the play does not endorse the fighter as it plainly does endorse the outdoorsman and the artisan. The prophet of violence is Ben, and his ultimate primogeniture is not the redeemed Biff but the lost Happy, who seems destined to remain a sexual predator and a frustrated failure in business. Contrastingly, Biff chooses a vocation which does not require or encourage him to be violent.

Willy Loman's concept of himself as a transmitter, one in a line of patriarchs who together unify several generations of Lomans, is extremely crucial, for, as we have seen, the struggle within each of his sons is the struggle of conflicting elements of their heritage. Dishonesty, avarice, self-deception, and conceit, as well as the love of nature, the need of real and fulfilling work, and the taste for violence, are all explicitly or implicity transmitted and nurtured by Willy. As we watch *Death of a Salesman*, we become convinced that some of these transmissions are evil and that others are at best mixed blessings, and eventually we come to question the very act of transmission, the fulfillment of the patriarchal role.

Willy scarcely knew his own father, and when his much older brother arrives at the Loman home, Willy makes a father of him:

"Can't you stay a few days? You're just what I need, Ben, because I—I have a fine position here, but I—well, Dad left when I was such a baby and I never had a chance to talk to him and I still feel—kind of temporary about myself." As we have seen, Willy's acceptance of Ben's teachings is disastrous. Another treacherous patriarch is Willy's former boss, old man Wagner, whom Willy calls "a prince, . . . a masterful man." Though Wagner made "promises" to Willy, Willy is cast out, penniless, after thirty-four years in the Wagners' service. Willy is a patriarch to his own sons throughout their youth, but he, like Ben and old man Wagner, is also a betrayer, and his betrayal costs him his patriarchal status. Discovering Willy with "Miss Francis," young Biff begins to cry. Willy is harshly paternal in his efforts to calm Biff: "Now stop crying and do as I say. I gave you an order, Biff, I gave you an order. Is that what you do when I give you an order?" Biff first ignores and then repudiates Willy, whose days of command are clearly over. Thus Biff is started on the long road to salvation. Happy, who never discovers Willy's infidelity and hence never comes to question Willy's assumptions about life, remains lost.

In assuming the role of patriarch, Willy is guilty of a kind of fatal *hubris*, for even those transmissions which are not evil may be misleading and useless. The view that appearance makes the man, for example, is not evil but false. Similarly, though Ben is unadmirable, his mode of life was once viable and necessary. But the shoot-first-and-ask-questions-later era of the American frontier is over, and even Ben, a generation older than Willy, must find adventure and success outside America. The transiency of Ben's day in history is brilliantly suggested by his gesture of repeatedly looking at his watch during his visits to the Lomans. In *Death of a Salesman* the viability of the patriarch's role is symbolized by the hirsuteness of Willy's father. The man of the next generation, Ben, wears only a mustache. Significantly, Willy himself is clean-shaven. A conclusive irony is that Charley, the anti-patriarch, whose "salvation is that he never took any interest in anything," rears a happy and fulfilled son. Unmanned in his ridiculous knickers, the man who can't handle tools fathers a manly lawyer who argues before the Supreme Court. Charley's success seems to tell us that all teaching must be cautious and implicit and that the young must define themselves.

Willy Loman was born as the American frontier era drew to a close. Growing up in a transitional period, he found no suitable identity. His civilization made the choice between Wall Street and Walden Pond both necessary and costly, and the man who chose Walden Pond often paid with his self-esteem. That civilization also made the career of a good craftsman somehow shameful. When any man may rise in society, not to do so becomes a crime. "Even your grandfather," Willy tells Biff, "was better than a carpenter." Industrial society, moreover, requires order. The wanderer is an outcast, and he who responds violently to the subtle men and implacable complexities of our time may go to jail. And he who would tell his children how to live may find his complex world sadly different from what he supposed it to be.

Death of a Salesman and Arthur Miller's Search for Style

Arthur K. Oberg

Arthur Miller's place in the contemporary theatre is based so exclusively upon the kind of social or public play he writes that the distinction of his language has been given small attention. When a play like *Death of a Salesman* has been considered for its speech, it has been dismissed as "bad poetry."[1] Although both Miller and Tennessee Williams have had plays directed and staged by Elia Kazan, critics tend to maximize the essential difference of their writing. In the established image, Miller's art is masculine and craggy; Williams', poetic and delicate. Such generalizations are not unjustifiable, but they obscure problems that Miller and Williams share and have attempted to solve in their respective dramas. For all of Miller's obverse comments on poetic poetry or the mood play,[2] his entire dramatic career has been an effort to get beyond a limited realism and a confining prose. Like Williams, he is in search of a style that will allow for an unusually expressive speech. And his use of a narrator in *A View from the Bridge* and his breakdown of time and space sequences in *Death of a Salesman* and *After the Fall* have been attempts at creating occasions when such language may be possible.

Miller's own comments and writings on the drama can be blamed for many of the unfavorable considerations that his dramatic prose has evoked. Miller is too harsh in insisting upon

Arthur K. Oberg, "*Death of a Salesman* and Arthur Miller's Search for Style," *Criticism*, 9 (1967), 303–11. Reprinted by permission of Wayne State University Press.

[1] Eric Bentley, *In Search of Theater* (New York, 1957), p. 82.

[2] Arthur Miller, "Introduction," *Collected Plays* (New York: The Viking Press, 1957), p. 12; "The Family in Modern Drama," *Atlantic Monthly*, CXCVII (April, 1956), 40.

the differences between drama and literature. In realizing that a play is more than a verbal art, Miller in the "Introduction" to his *Collected Plays* makes his point at the expense of undercutting what importance a text does and can possess.[3] There is an uncritical and confused use of words such as "poetic" and "social" that conceals how much concern with a distinctive language Miller's plays reveal. A distrust of poetic poetry by Miller is understandable in view of the abortive verse play revival and the suspicion of audiences toward emotion and poetry, a suspicion evidenced by a drift toward *"indiscriminate* understatement"[4] in the theatre. But Miller's recorded devaluation of the language of a play is at strange odds with his continued excursions into finding an adequate stage speech in his work.

What the body of Miller's plays confirms is a situation that O'Neill found in the theatre many years ago and that continues to perplex the American dramatist—a lack of an established and available idiom. An interest in and employment of dialects— whether Irish, tough, sex, or alcoholic conversation[5]—became O'Neill's response to this situation. It recurs with slight variation in Miller's archaic Puritan speech in *The Crucible* and in his varieties of American localese in other plays. We are given dialogue that is different from what we are accustomed to hear, but always sufficiently recognizable for comprehension. Slices of life are presented that alternately provide us with the pleasures of hearing familiar speech and unfamiliar (or, to its users, *more* familiar) vernacular. Whereas Shakespeare's use of dialect only pointed to the presence of some standard stage speech in the background, its use by O'Neill and Miller indicates the contemporary absence of an established idiom. Back in 1923 Ezra Pound objected to dialects as "a usual form of evasion in modern drama";[6] but such a judgment ignores considerations of their decorum for particular

[3]Miller, "Introduction," pp. 3–5.

[4]Louis MacNeice, "Introductory Note" to *Sunbeams in His Hat, The Dark Tower and Other Radio Scripts* (London, 1947), p. 70. American Group Theatre in the thirties and Actor's Studio today, assuming that acting neither begins nor ends in speech, testify to the fact that even acting has been influenced by the drift toward understatement; on the assumptions of method acting see Eric Bentley, *The Dramatic Event* (New York, 1954), p. 173.

[5]Bentley, *The Dramatic Event*, p. 32; *In Search of Theater*, pp. 225, 232; Kenneth Tynan, *Curtains* (New York, 1961), p. 203.

[6]Ezra Pound, February 1923 Paris Letter, *The Dial*, March 1923, p. 277.

plays and of the competence with which they are employed. And
the continuing use, for example, of Southern speech and slangy
colloquialism in the American drama reveals both partial solu-
tions and impasses unsolved.

Miller comes to a theatre whose audiences are daily glutted with
words from the commercial media. He accepts the embarrassment of audiences before emotive writing while affirming the right
of the theatre to make people both think and feel. Although poets
and poetry are joked about in several of his plays, language is
undercut only so that it may be possible at all. Like Shaw or
Arnold Wesker or Jack Richardson, Miller presents the poet as
dolt or dreamer.[7] And, like them, he then goes on to use words as
if he had forgotten the difficulties involved. In the face of the
absurd impossibility of finding even adequate words, Miller drives
on to accomplish what would not seem allowed.

If the situation in the American theatre is as complex and
discouraging as has been indicated—the lack of an established
idiom, the suspicions of an audience toward poetry and emotion—
Miller's various attempts toward solving the problems of text take
on a new meaning. They suggest as extensive an experiment as
Eliot's with the verse line. Although Miller's revision of *A View from
the Bridge* ended his one attempt at using a verse line in the theatre,
each of his plays and nondramatic works relates to a lifetime
search for a distinctive style. Miller's approximations of Western
Speech in *The Misfits* and of seventeenth century speech in *The
Crucible* solved this problem only for these particular works. Like
Eliot after *Murder in the Cathedral*, Miller uncovers in his dramatic
career an effort to forge a speech that would generally serve for
whatever play he might happen to write. In *Death of a Salesman* and
the plays that follow—with the exception of *The Crucible* whose style
becomes an interruption, usable for one play—Miller picks up
where the dialogue of *All My Sons* left off.

From Miller's earliest plays to *Incident at Vichy* there is a distinctive speech which, regardless of ostensible setting or background
of characters, is based upon a New York idiom that often has
recognizably Jewish inflection (e.g. the rising rhythms of "Does it

---

[7]An interesting consideration of Shaw's Octavius and Marchbanks as "unintentionally sentimental" is given by Kenneth Muir, "Verse and Prose," *Contemporary Theatre* ("Stratford-upon-Avon Studies" 4) (London, 1962), p. 103.

take more guts to stand here the rest of my life ringing up a zero?").[8] Miller has an ear for speech that can be heard in any of the New York boroughs, for rhythms that have filtered down into Gentile conversation many miles from the city. Beginning with a particular speech, Miller arrives at something that approaches an American idiom to the extent that it exposes a colloquialism characterized by unusual image, spurious lyricism, and close-ended cliché. One has the impression of characters cheering themselves up with a speech that is counterpointed by what we already know as audience about them. For Miller, it is a conscious selection from the speech that he has known and heard from childhood through which he exposes such discrepancies, particularly rents in the American dream. And it is in *Death of a Salesman* that he perfects this idiom to allow for a more successful revelation of complex character than in any other play he wrote.

The language of *Death of a Salesman* has characteristics that link it with all of Miller's work. Miller has a talent for using words and phrases as leitmotifs ("He's liked, but he's not—well liked"), for writing what approaches but is less obvious and short than set speech. Linda and Willy's occasional soliloquy-like musings relate to this kind of patterned speech that typifies Miller's earlier and later plays:

> The cats in that alley are practical, the bums who ran away when we were fighting were practical. Only the dead ones weren't practical. But now I'm practical, and I spit on myself, I'm going away. I'm going now.[9]

> No, no. Now let me instruct you. We cannot look to superstition in this. The Devil is precise; the marks of his presence are definite as stone, and I must tell you all that I shall not proceed unless you are prepared to believe me if I should find no bruise of hell upon her.[10]

Similarly, prominent striking images ("He was so humiliated he nearly limped when he came in" [p. 211]; "All the talk that went

---

[8]Arthur Miller, *Death of a Salesman, Collected Plays*, p. 212. Quotations from *Death of a Salesman* are hereafter given in the text and are taken from this edition.

[9]Arthur Miller, *All My Sons, Collected Plays*, p. 123.

[10]Arthur Miller, *The Crucible, Collected Plays*, p. 252.

across those two beds, huh? Our whole lives" [p. 137], recall the earmarks of other plays, dialogue that hesitates between mixed metaphor and metaphysical concern:

> Frank is right—every man does have a star. The star of one's honesty.[11]

> This society will not be a bag to swing around your head, Mr. Putnam.[12]

> Quentin, don't hold the future like a vase—touch now, touch me! I'm here, and it's now![13]

> You'd better ram a viewpoint up your spine or you'll break in half.[14]

Miller here reveals three things: a knack of linking an abstract and a concrete in metaphor, a pressing of metaphor to visual incongruity or cartoon-like animation, and a preference for letting an audience bear away one or two vivid images in contrast to the *copia* of a playwright like Christopher Fry. While implicit attitudes toward kinds of rhetoric possible within a contemporary play would further link *Death of a Salesman* with the body of Miller's work, it is the particular density of a familiar Miller rhetoric that gives *Death of a Salesman* a feel that none of his other plays achieves. And the density is dictated by the enclosed situation in which the main character is found.

When Miller undertook in *Death of a Salesman* to present the plight of Willy Loman, he offered a reexamination of radical aspects of the American dream. The Lomans, never a family of adults, gradually and painfully attest to discrepancies in the American success myth, discrepancies that their lives from time to time can no longer hide. What Willy and his sons and what Charley and Bernard indicate in their respective failures and successes is the presence of arbitrary gods. Willy clings to them as he is beaten by them, and Miller's "requiem" confirms them as a part of the territory. For Loman, they are both equipment for living and vestments of death. As the play moves through its rhythms of euphoric elation and relentless despair, Miller employs

[11]Miller, *All My Sons, Collected Plays*, p. 118.
[12]Miller, *The Crucible, Collected Plays*, p. 244.
[13]Arthur Miller, *After the Fall* (New York, 1964), p. 100.
[14]Arthur Miller, *Incident at Vichy* (New York, 1965), p. 31.

a speech that would uphold these values by embedding them in outworn, formulated clichés commonly negatively phrased: "Never fight fair with a stranger, boy," "nobody's worth nothin dead," "No man only needs a little salary." But elsewhere there is language that draws near to "something of a poetic tinge," "a great air of something like poetry," "a kind of poetry";[15]

> The world is an oyster, but you don't crack it open on a mattress." (p. 152)

> When a deposit bottle is broken you don't get your nickel back. (p. 154)

> Everybody likes a kidder, but nobody lends him money. (p. 168)

But even when Miller attempts to revitalize language we detect one and the same process here going on—the reduction of living to a set of adages, whether familiar or not.

There are two actions concurrently running in *Death of a Salesman* and related to this reduction of living to cliché. One is a process of exposing and opening up, showing differences in the characters' ideals and lives; the other, an undermining of their clichéd and commonplace lives. The first movement is most obviously reflected in images of stripping down that recur in the play. When Willy protests that "you can't eat the orange and throw the peel away—a man is not a piece of fruit!" (p. 181), he ironically confirms Linda's early adage that "life is a casting off" (p. 133). In context, Linda's words sounded only like readily available consolation, but the brute honesty behind them becomes clear in the remark of Loman's uttered later in the play. Willy's and Linda's lines, when played against one another from such a distance, force an honesty that much of their talk would hide.

Further dislocations in the American dream become prominent in Miller's reconsideration of the ideals of athletic prowess, male friendship, popularity, unpopular success. A society that jointly praises the democratic ideal and the exceptional individual is seen to be schizoid in its confusion of opportunity, talent, and abstract right. Against the process of exposing these often contradictory ideals, Miller sets the weight of the entire clichéd speech of the

[15]George Jean Nathan, Eleanor Clark, Harold Clurman, "Reviews of *Death of a Salesman,*" *Two Modern American Tragedies: Reviews and Criticism of Death of a Salesman and A Streetcar Named Desire*, ed. John D. Hurrell (New York, 1961), pp. 57, 64, 66.

play. What the characters say is an effort in conservation, an
upholding of a societal structure that has made it less and less
likely for the small man to succeed. Social and economic statement is involved, but Miller goes beyond this statement in presenting Loman as a man not only trapped by his culture, but
growing ineffectual and old. Willy and his sons have reached a
time in life when they can live neither together nor apart. Although
Willy's feelings of loss and impermanence are intensified and
partly caused by his lack of success, his predicament has more
complex origins. Willy is a man of slipping powers, locked in the
past. Pathetically, in the face of declining earning power and
approaching death, he would keep what he does not have and
provide for what is not allowed.

The passages of *Death of a Salesman* using intentionally spurious,
lyrical metaphor and suggestive of the kind of counterpointing
found in Chekhov and O'Neill provide their own charm and force:

> That's why I thank Almighty God you're both built like Adonises.
> (p. 146)

> Like a young god, Hercules—something like that. And the sun, the
> sun all around him. Remember how he waved to me? (p. 171)

> Miss Forsythe, you've just seen a prince walk by. A fine, troubled
> prince. A hardworking, unappreciated prince. A pal, you under-
> stand? A good companion. Always for his boys. (p. 204).

Such princely metaphor arises in moments of euphoria and functions much like the pal or buddy talk of Willy and his sons or like
the diminutive language which ironically becomes *more* sentimental
in seeking to reduce the sentimentality involved:

> A small man can be just as exhausted as a great man. (p. 163)

> Be loving to him. Because he's only a little boat looking for a
> harbor. (p. 176)

Yet, for all this recognizably stylized speech which is reminiscent
of other of Miller's plays, it is finally the fragmented wisdom of
cliché, shored against Willy's ruin, that defines the language of the
play. Miller relentlessly pins down by means of New York dialect,
and with a talent akin to Pinter's, the shrinkage and simplification
of living made possible by cliché. The Lomans in *Death of a
Salesman* use formulated wisdom to hold off the night when they
will have to acknowledge what they evade, unhappiness and

failure. In contrast, Charley and his son use this wisdom to reflect the constricted perspective and unrestricted ambition often necessary in the pursuit of success. "The sky's the limit." "If at first you don't succeed, . . ." "One must go in to fetch a diamond cut." "The only thing you got in this world is what you can sell." In their clichés, Miller's characters reveal both partial, pragmatically Puritan truths and denials of what an audience sees before their eyes— that all Americans cannot and do not succeed, that men do sometimes cry, that having sons is no guarantee of masculinity or success. Although Willy repeats that "the woods are burning," he refuses to locate what he only vaguely feels and knows. With the exception of those moments when honesty is pleaded for, Willy maintains and is maintained by speech that excludes it.

Behind the reduction of being to a set of recurrent adages, we hear the helplessness, hopelessness and frustration of words that can neither cheer Loman up nor improve his predicament. These time-worn phrases became useless and superfluous a long time ago. But they continue to be repeated, and almost religiously, by the characters in the play. Like a charm, they are an evasion and fear of redefining and delineating what has occurred. In the familiarly colloquial and deceptively self-sufficient clichés of the American dream, all is caught and held. The rhythms of the play, recognizably those of lower middle-class New York, could be heard across the country, with variations only in inflection and phrasing and specific cliché. In these rhythms Miller gives expression to a specifically American process or tendency to talk against facts of loneliness and loss, the fact of time-space breaking down under the pressures of memory and madness. He gives voice to rents in the American dream.

Unlike the plays of O'Neill or Williams where much of the power derives from "the cost to the dramatist of what he handled,"[16] *Death of a Salesman* relies upon a greater distancing and objectivity of the playwright. Whatever "otiose breast-beating"[17] occurs is either so subordinated to the play's elusive reticence or so much of an expression of a kind of emotional cliché that the impression is one of a succession of pre-verbalized states that were reinforced in the theatre by the poetic lighting, music, and staging of Kazan. As Willy and the other characters aspire toward greater truthfulness,

---

[16]Stark Young, *Immortal Shadows* (New York, 1948), p. 65.
[17]Tynan, *Curtains*, p. 260.

they are held back by a stylized, cliché-ridden language that encourages evasion as it seeks to bring back a time when Thomas Edison and B. F. Goodrich and J. P. Morgan were still possible. That *Death of a Salesman* is both a document and requiem to this time explains the play's language, if it also provides a circular defense for that style.

However suitable the density of cliché finally is for Miller's purposes in *Death of a Salesman*, we are left with the general impression of a text that is undistinguished and flat. Arguments offered earlier for an intentionally spurious lyricism or for an unusual turn of cliché relate to moments in the play that are too few to absolve the longer stretches of Miller's prose. The play's text, although far from "bad poetry," tellingly moves toward the status of poetry without ever getting there.[18] Although the reasons given for this situation go a long way to explain the quality of the text, to let the case rest on the attitudes of the audience either toward poetry or toward emotion explains one matter only to ignore the power that the play continues to elicit on the stage. That the distinction of the play is not primarily verbal returns us to our earlier considerations of the achievement of *Death of a Salesman* as one of style—style as rhythm, rhythm as style.

As we noted, Miller in *Death of a Salesman* uses a stylistically clichéd language, based on the inflection of a New York Jewish speech and rising to a peculiarly American idiom, to reveal the disparities between Willy's pipe dreams and what has occurred, alternating rhythms of elation and despair dramatically and artistically realize what life less coherently and concentratedly presents. As a result, the strength of the speech of the Lomans resides in its pressing toward what it must never become. Never a poetry of full light, it is a prose characterized by clichés that guy rhythm as they create a style. Here, the distinctiveness of the play lies. In looking beyond the clichéd words of *Death of a Salesman* to the rhythms of the speech and to what the clichés would hide, we draw near to the kind of appreciation that vaudeville, another popular art, must exact—when what is central are not the words spoken but the "bounce" of the music hall line.

[18]See the critical consensus in note 15.

Death of a Salesman

B. S. Field, Jr.

One of the things one looks for in any play, be it comedy, tragedy, or garrago, is the propriety of the catastrophe. How does the final disaster, the embarrassment or the agony of the protagonist, which it is the play's business to recount, stand as an appropriate consequence to the protagonist's sin, his fault, his *hamartia?* A critic's struggle to "explain" a play is often in large measure simply the attempt to verbalize that relationship, to describe the poetic justice of the play, the propriety of matching that *hamartia* with those consequences.

In Arthur Miller's *Death of a Salesman*, how does Willy's catastrophe stand as a poetically just consequence of his *hamartia?* Many answers to that question have been suggested, and many of them help in some measure to describe why the play succeeds. My thesis is modest enough. It is offered not in any attempt to displace other explanations, but as an addition to the multiple cause-effect relationships in that modern drama. Willy committed a crime for which he is justly punished.

The criticism of *Death of a Salesman* falls into two schools, that which feels it necessary to explain why the play fails, and that which feels it necessary to explain why the play succeeds. Since it seems to me that the play succeeds, and since it seems fruitless to attempt to argue people into liking something that they do not like, let what follows be addressed exclusively to those who agree that the play succeeds.

For it does succeed. In the court that has final provenance in such a case, the stage, the verdict is that *Death of a Salesman* is a success. Most of the adverse criticism of this play, and there is a lot

B.S. Field, Jr., *"Death of a Salesman," Twentieth Century Literature* 18 (1972), 19–24. Reprinted by permission of the publisher.

of it, tries to argue that because the play is not unified and coherent in the way a classical tragedy is coherent, it is a failure, not only as a tragedy, but as a work of art of any kind.[1] Alfred Schwarz has pointed out while reviewing the discussions of this issue by Hebbel, Büchner, Luckács, and by Miller himself, that there is not even a theoretical necessity for a modern tragedy to be unified and coherent in the same ways we have learned to expect in a classic tragedy.[2] A modern realistic tragedy, even in theory, is a multiple device. Such tragedy is anchored not in eternal conditions, as man's relation to fate, but in the immediate and ever shifting conditions of men's relations with each other and with their institutions. Thus a modern play, to be successful, even to be effective tragedy, needs not even theoretically to be singular. On the contrary, according to the poetic that Schwarz describes, a modern drama will present manifold causes of a manifold catastrophe illustrating a manifold theme.[3]

It is clear enough from all the criticism that *Death of a Salesman* has a theme that is open to various interpretations. One large group insists that it is, or ought to be, about Willy's isolation from nature. Others point out that Willy suffers from a lack of love, a loss of identity, a worship of the False God of Personality.[4] The

[1] Representative negative judgments of the play are to be found in Eric Bentley, "Better than Europe?" *In Search of Theater* (New York, 1953), pp. 84–88, reprinted in John D. Hurrell, ed., *Two Modern American Tragedies* (New York, 1961), pp. 131–134; Eleanor Clark, review of *Death of a Salesman, Partisan Review* XVI (June, 1949), 631–635, reprinted in Hurrell, pp. 61–64; Richard J. Foster, "Confusion and Tragedy: the Failure of Miller's *Salesman,*" in Hurrell, pp. 82–91; John V. Hagopagian, "The *Salesman's* Two Cases," *Modern Drama,* VI (1963), 117–125; and in Joseph Hynes, "Attention must be Paid . . ." *College English,* XIII (1961–62), 574–578.

[2] Alfred Schwarz, "Towards a Poetic of Modern Realistic Tragedy," *Modern Drama,* IX (1966), 136–146.

[3] Dennis Welland, *Arthur Miller* (London, 1961), presents a very sensible and balanced analysis of *Death of a Salesman* working from just this assumption about the play's multiplicity of causes and effects.

[4] Representative analysis of this kind are to be found in Barclay W. Bates, "The Lost Past in *Death of a Salesman,*" *Modern Drama,* XI (1968–69), 164–172; Sister M. Bettina, SSND, "Willy Loman's Big Brother Ben: the Tragic Insight in *Death of a Salesman,*" *Modern Drama,* IV (1962), 409–412; Barry Gross, "Peddlers and Pioneers in *Death of a Salesman,*" *Modern Drama,* VII (1964–65), 405–410; Sheila Huftel, *Arthur Miller: The Burning Glass* (New York, 1965); Stephen Lawrence, "The Right Dream in Miller's *Death of a Salesman,*" *College English,* XXV (1964), 547–548; Leonard Moss, *Arthur Miller* (New York, 1967); Edward Murray, *Arthur Miller,*

causes of Willy's disaster are presented with equal variety: he is defeated by society; he is too weak and immoral for any social conditions; he once made a wrong choice of careers; he married a woman who tried to stifle his sense of adventure; or simply that he got too old. And the condition that constitutes Willy's catastrophe is also variously described: he suffered a miserable and pointless death; he suffered the agony of seeing that he had worthless sons; he suffered the agony of the whole twenty-four hours of insane self-torture which takes up the supposed "real" time of the play's performance; or simply that he had a miserable funeral.

It is pointless to argue that because one of these can be a correct analysis, the others must be wrong, even though in Miller's play, in the "Requiem" which closes it, Charley, Biff, Happy, and perhaps Linda, too, argue as if their explanations of Willy's catastrophe were mutually exclusive. They may all be right, even Linda, who says, "I don't understand," that is, that it is inexplicable.

Elements of the play that have not received the attention from critics that they deserve are those scenes which display Willy training his sons. Bates suggests that one of the roles in which Willy tries to function is that of the "dutiful patriarchal male intent upon transmitting complex legacies from his forebears to his progeny."[5] The episodes which support that generalization, however, do not indicate that Willy has any clear ideas what legacy he has received from his forebears. He speaks vaguely of his father who was "better than a carpenter," who made flutes, and in the scenes with Ben he pleads with his brother to tell him something that he can transmit.

> Please tell about Dad. I want my boys to hear. I want them to know the kind of stock they spring from. All I remember is a man with a big beard, and I was in Mamma's lap, sitting around a fire . . .[6] (p. 48)

Dramatist (New York, 1967); Brian Parker, "Point of View in Arthur Miller's *Death of a Salesman,*" *University of Toronto Quarterly*, XXXV (1966), 144–57, reprinted in Robert W. Corrigan, ed., *Arthur Miller, A Collection of Critical Essays* (Englewood Cliffs, 1969), pp. 95–109.

[5] Bates, p. 164.

[6] Numbers in parentheses are page numbers of quotations from Arthur Miller, *Death of a Salesman* (New York, 1949).

Later he complains to Ben of his fears, that "sometimes I'm afraid that I'm not teaching them the right kind of—Ben, what should I teach them?"

Part of this tragedy is that what he has taught them does not look to him like what he wanted them to have learned. Miller drops suggestions into the first part of the play that while Biff is a charismatic young man, he has also the makings of an amoral punk. In the bedroom with Happy near the beginning of the play, Biff speaks of going to see Bill Oliver.

> *Biff:* I wonder if Oliver still thinks I stole that carton of basketballs.
> *Happy:* Oh, he probably forgot about that long ago. It's almost ten years. You're too sensitive. Anyway, he didn't really fire you.
> *Biff:* Well, he was going to. I think that's why I quit. I was never sure whether he knew or not. (p. 26)

Biff's first speech suggests that he feels aggrieved at being suspected, his second speech suggests that Oliver was right to suspect him. Moments later in the script Willy brings home a new punching bag. Then Biff shows off the new football that he has "borrowed" from the locker room. Willy, laughing, tells him that he has to return it:

> *Happy:* I told you he wouldn't like it!
> *Biff:* (Angrily) Well, I'm bringing it back!
> *Willy:* (Stopping the incipient argument, to HAPPY) Sure, he's gotta practice with a regulation ball, doesn't he? (To BIFF) Coach'll probably congratulate you on your initiative. (p. 30)

The boys are not mean boys. Indeed, they are cheerful and eager. They carry Willy's bags in from the car. They help Linda carry up the wash. But they steal things, they cheat. Bernard complains that Biff doesn't study:

> *Willy:* Where is he? I'll whip him. I'll whip him!
> *Linda:* And he'd better give back that football, Willy, it's not nice.
> *Willy:* Biff! Where is he? Why is he taking everything? (p. 40)

Moments later in the script, Willy complains again:

> Loaded with it. Loaded! What is he stealing? He's giving it back, isn't he? Why is he stealing? What did I tell him? I never in my life told him anything but decent things. (p. 41)

Miller underscores these same issues again later on in the same act when Charley suggests that it is a poor idea to steal building materials, and, of course, again in the second half of the play when Biff walks out of Bill Oliver's office with Oliver's pen and then cannot go back and face the man.

> *Biff:* I took those balls years ago, now I walk in with his fountain pen? That clinches it, don't you see? I can't face him like that!

Among the more famous analyses of *Death of a Salesman* is the one published by a psychiatrist while the original production was still on the Broadway stage. Daniel E. Schneider saw the play as an expression of Willy's aggression against his older brother Ben, as Happy's aggressions against Biff. Schneider speaks of the meeting of the father and his sons in the bar as a "totem feast," the whole play as "an irrational Oedipal bloodbath," of Willy's sudden need to go to the bathroom in that barroom sequence as "castration panic," and points out the possible sexual significance of that stolen pen, those stolen basketballs and footballs. Most commentators on *Death of a Salesman* seem to have found Schneider's analysis of the play of little use. At any rate, few of them mentioned him. And indeed Schneider's attempt to point out a pattern seems perhaps a bit forced, that is, a bit psycho-analytic. But he makes some telling points.[7]

There is a pattern, one I think, that has not been pointed out before. It is worth remembering how often, in scenes involving Willy's training of his sons, that balls, footballs, basketballs, punching bags, appear. If Schneider's suggestion is valid that these balls are images of a concern with castration, the implication follows that Willy is guilty of a crime that can serve as the *hamartia* for which his catastrophe is poetically just.

Willy's crime is that he has tried to mould his sons in his own image, that he has turned them into wind-bags and cry-babies. They are not sexually impotent, no more than Willy is, but they

---

[7]Daniel E. Schneider, "Play of Dreams," *Theater Arts* (October, 1949), pp. 18–21.

are impotent in a larger sense. Happy complains of the meaninglessness of his life.

> Sometimes I sit in my apartment—all alone. And I think of the rent
> I'm paying. And it's crazy. But then, it's what I always wanted. My
> own apartment, a car, and plenty of women. And still, goddammit,
> I'm lonely. (p. 23)

The boys are not impotent sexually, but morally and socially.
Willy himself has no basis for making moral choices. It is not so
much that he chooses or has chosen evil, but that he has no idea
how to choose at all. Everyone, himself included, is constantly
contradicting him. He lives in a morally incoherent universe, an
incoherence that is the most striking element of the play which
describes his torments. And because he is morally incapacitated,
he is socially incapacitated. Everything is against him. The city is
killing him. The competition is killing him. He cannot get along
with the son he loves most. The very seeds he plants no longer
grow. Nothing he does has any consequences. He simply cannot
make anything happen.

One may, in describing a person like Willy who has no "character," in the vulgate employed in Miller's dialogue, say of Willy
that "he's got no balls." And neither have his sons. Willy's efforts
to mould these boys in his own image have not been a failure but a
success. They are just like him. They offer two aspects of the same
personality, Happy taking more after his mother, perhaps, but
both sharing the same defect with their father. They cannot make
anything happen. They are morally and socially castrated.

To the other causes of Willy's catastrophe, then, to Willy's weakness, his incompetence to deal with a society too cruel to pay him
the attention that he cannot wrest from it with his own strength, to
his isolation from nature, to his incapacity to explain his own
situation to himself, to his feelings of a loss of identity, of spiritual
dryness, of lack of love, to his erroneous worship at the altar of
personality, I suggest we may add to all these his crime: he has
made moral eunuchs of his own sons. His is a criminality, a
hamartia, for which the punishment, that miserable life, that miserable death, and that miserable funeral too, are appropriate and
decorous consequences.

Who Am I? . . . A Re-Investigation of Arthur Miller's *Death of a Salesman*

Charlotte F. Otten

I shivered as I hurried through the streets of downtown Nijmegen in the Netherlands. It was February and damp as an Italian dungeon here today. I was too chilled to hesitate for even a moment to glance into the bookshop windows. Suddenly I stopped dead. There, in that attractive bookshop window, stood Willy Loman of *Death of a Salesman.* He obviously was not sizzling on his launching pad—this was ten years after Arthur Miller had hit the Broadway moon with him. But what I could not really understand was what *Death of a Salesman* was doing in an obscure European city among people whose ideals were so different from Willy Loman's that they could not talk the same essential language. I had never attributed universal quality to *Death of a Salesman,* and I wondered what a Dutchman, who is constantly waging his own personal war against materialism, would do with a man like Willy Loman, who had only a Personality-Dollar Ideal. Could the Dutch understand Willy, a two-bit-an-hour American salesman, an insignificant little man with an employment problem? They would have to know all about American advertising and selling, I thought, in order to find Willy the slightest bit interesting, let alone understand him. Or not? Could Willy speak to every person of every country of every age?

Upon re-reading *Death of a Salesman* I recognized immediately, of course, that although it is particularly American in flavor, it is projected against the deep philosophical forces of all times and that it takes its place right next to Sophoclean and Shakespearean drama; that although it speaks in the modern American idiom, it is

Charlotte F. Otten, "Who Am I? . . . A Re-investigation of Arthur Miller's *Death of a Salesman*," *Cresset,* 26 (February, 1963), 11–13. Reprinted by permission of the publisher.

not only colloquial and suburban, it is profound and universal.

Now to find out who Willy Loman is; and so back to the bare statistics. Name—Willy Loman; age—63; residence—Brooklyn; wife—Linda; sons—Biff and Happy; occupation—salesman, New England territory; years of service—45; average income—$70, income diminishing; health—good. There stood the essential information, dull as any application blank. And still I did not know who Willy was.

Jocasta's Sons

I operated on the assumption that if you want to know who a man is, find out who his family is. I decided to look at his wife first (wives have a way of being miniature-husbands). There stands Linda Loman, mending a silk stocking. She will never know that the silk stocking is the symbol of Willy's unfaithfulness to her—the silk stockings which he gave to "the laughing woman," the "woman taken in adultery" in Boston. We hear Linda saying all the inane things a wife is inclined to say when her husband comes home from work: "Don't you feel well . . . you look terrible . . . I got a new kind of American-type cheese today. It's whipped."

Always Linda has to pin down Willy financially; always she cannot pay the bills; yet always she helps him pretend that he is more successful than he really is. She will never admit that he is a failure. Linda will not look at Willy face to face, and so she does not really see him at all. Full sight is death, she knows, and so she cannot even remove the rubber pipe Willy has connected to the nipple on the gas pipe for suicide. But one thing Linda knows and admits: Biff, her older son, holds Willy's life in his hands. Willy is somewhere deep inside Biff. The power of life or death is his for Willy. Once, timidly, she asks, "Willy, dear, what has he got against you?" But in that moving scene, when Biff begins to tell the truth to Willy, Linda pleads, almost screams, "Stop it!"

This is Linda. She can be described as ordinary, loving, a blind leader of the blind. But isn't Linda vaguely familiar? Hasn't she appeared in dramatic literature before? She is not pushy, aggressive, ambitious like Lady Macbeth; she is rather like Jocasta, the wife of Oedipus the King. I could hear Jocasta saying, "For God's love let us have no more questioning! . . . May you never learn who you are." What a strange affinity. Jocasta, brilliant fifth-century B.C. queen of Thebes, is giving precisely the same advice to her husband, the noble King Oedipus, as Linda Loman, mousy twentieth-century Brooklyn housewife, is giving to her husband Willy, the unsuccessful salesman. Although the external circumstances vary greatly and twenty-five centuries separate these women, yet they are sisters of the heart. They try to prevent their husbands from asking the fatal question, "Who am I?"

Back to the Loman family. There is Happy, the younger son. He is easy to analyze. He is "confused and hard-skinned," a coarser, obtuser Willy. Happy is even blinder than Willy. Happy sees not a glimmer of light. He is in the totally-blind, born-blind category. His father Willy is in the partially-blind category; and that is harder. When Biff confronts Happy with the consistent falsehood of their lives, Happy shouts, "We always told the truth!" Happy is completely self-centered and the self-centered person cannot know his *self.* If he could not know himself, how could he know his father? At Willy's grave he is still deluded. He says grandly, majestically, as only a very little immature boy would say it: "I'm gonna show you and everybody else that Willy Loman did not die in vain. He had a good dream. It's the only dream you can have— to come out number one-man. He fought it out here and this is where I'm gonna win it for him." This is a breath of hot air, if ever there was one. Happy makes no impression on anyone, except himself, and so he does not annoy or disturb or awaken Willy either.

But it is Biff who counts.

Biff, the older son, the son of the birthright, the son of Willy's dreams. On Biff Willy has heaped all his hopes and ambitions and the ideal of Success. Biff, when he played football in high school, looked "like a young god . . . Hercules . . ." to Willy. But Biff is no longer in high school and no longer playing football. He is thirty-four and amounts to a big zero. The vision of the young god has faded, and Willy says, "Not finding yourself at the age of thirty-four is a disgrace . . . he's a lazy bum." Willy wants him to be a god again, and he gives a last piece of desperate advice, "You're a salesman, and you don't know that."

There is more to Biff than meets the eye. Linda says to Biff, "It's when you come he's always the worst . . . When you write you're coming, he's all smiles, and talks about the future, and he's just wonderful. And then the closer you seem to come, the more shaky he gets, and then, by the time you get here, he's arguing, and he seems angry at you . . . Why are you so hateful to each other?" Biff is the only one who knows who Willy is: "I know he's a fake and he doesn't like anybody around who knows . . . Don't touch me you—liar! You fake! You phony little fake!" In utter moral desperation Biff blurts out, "You're going to hear the truth—what you are and what I am."

In a way Biff seems almost medieval, like Truth or Conscience with a capital letter. And still is this Biff—the twentieth century American no-good in a morality role? No, he goes farther back, back past A.D. to B.C. Back to Oedipus again. I must say that I was startled to find that Biff looked for all the world like Teiresias, Oedipus's enemy-friend. And isn't that precisely Biff, Willy's enemy-son, with the strong hate-love motif? Who is it that knows the truth about Oedipus, the horrible, bloody truth? It is Teiresias. Oedipus pleads with him for the truth: "In God's name we all beg you—" but Teiresias says, "No, I will never tell you what I know. Now it is my misery; then, it would be yours." And when Teiresias finally blurts out the truth and tells Oedipus that it is he who has murdered his father and married his mother and that the whole city suffers because of his guilty acts, then Oedipus rages at Teiresias: "You sightless, witless, senseless, mad old man!" And it sounds like Willy and Biff all over again.

Oedipus and Teiresias

Teiresias and Biff Loman in the same breath; yet, do they not stand together and stand for the same thing? There is an odd relationship between Biff and Willy which runs strangely parallel to Teiresias and Oedipus. In a twentieth-century drama about a "hard-working drummer who landed in the ash can" there is a prophet, a Sophoclean seer. He is Biff. Biff and Teiresias stand together and point the finger with the prophet Nathan and say, "Look within. Thou art the man." They are the same.

And Willy himself. Linda, Happy, Biff—all lead to Willy. He is a salesman, or what is left of a salesman, or what is left of a man. He wanted to be a great salesman; and because he wanted it so bad he thought he was a great salesman. If ever he hints at failure, he blames others, "People don't seem to take to me," but quickly he shifts back to his dream of being a great salesman and says in the same breath, "I'm very well liked in Hartford."

Although he is sixty-three years old, Willy is an adolescent: he sees only the dream and not the reality. When his friend Charley asks, "When . . . are you going to grow up?" Willy shouts, "You big ignoramus, if you say that to me again I'll rap you one." If only Willy had been willing to admit that he was more of a carpenter than a salesman, that there was more of him in that front stoop than in all the sales he had ever made. If only he had known who he was. But he did not. In a banal, final act of self-delusion, he decides to commit suicide for the $20,000 insurance money he can ꝟ leave to Biff: "He'll worship me for it." Willy rejects Biff's moral role and thereby loses his life. Oedipus accepts Teiresias's verdict and loses his life that he may find it.

Oedipus and Willy

Oedipus the King and Willy the Salesman—what do they have in common? Each is the hero of a great play. But how different the two worlds which they inhabit. Their worlds have nothing in common. Oedipus lived in a world where he could wrestle against principalities and powers, against the rulers of the darkness of this world, against spiritual wickedness in high places. Oedipus lived in a world of big virtues and big vices, in a world where sin counted. It was a world of Guilt and Retribution; Grace had not yet arrived. Oedipus is King: he is king in this kind of world. Oedipus could ask the question, "Who am I?" and hope to find an answer. All he had to do was find his relationship to the gods, to those who predestined his actions. Oedipus sees himself clearly, stares at himself and at his awful guilt, and he pierces and stabs his eyes till the tears run red and he hides his face from himself and from his children who are also his brothers. And still he cannot pluck out his inner eyes, and always they bore into his soul and seek out the stark horrible reality. And eventually, although the guilt is great and the question "Who am I?" is all hectic red and bloody, eventually he knows who he is—and there is peace. Peace on earth for himself and good will to all men in Thebes.

But what about Willy? Surely he had not murdered his father and was not husband to his mother. He had committed a little humdrum adultery, to be sure, but what is a little adultery on the part of one insignificant bundle of atoms (called man) in an expanding universe? Willy's twentieth century world cannot tolerate the question, "Who am I?" Willy cannot look in or out or up. No need to plunge a dagger into his sightless eyes. He is blind in an unseeing world. Willy can only cling to his intangible dream and try vainly to clutch it, and always he cannot grasp it. His face bears the marks of his great un-successes, his unfulfilled desires, and Biff can only say, "I can't bear to look at his face." It is the face that shows. And Willy cannot bear to look in a mirror nor face to face at Biff, for then he shall know and be known.

Willy Loman's world is the world of the split-atom and the split-personality. Willy, most of his acquaintances would say, ought to see a psychiatrist: his troubles are psychological, not moral. After all, let's not pretend that Willy really counts in this modern universe. This is not the simple, orderly, stately world of Oedipus the King, of Guilt and Retribution. This is not a Christian world either, where God becomes man, wipes out his guilt, and tells him who he is. Willy's is a post-Greek, post-Christian world which is growing from the inside out; the cosmic forces are stirring within the earth and man is trying to hurl himself off his earth; and what is man, or what is Willy Loman, that the earth or the cosmic forces should be mindful of him? Willy is a chestless man, his world has cut out his heart, and he is doomed to be a stranger to himself forever. He can never know who he is.

Willy is a product-seller and a product-user, nothing more. Willy is a salesman with no place to go except to hell and no one to turn to except himself and himself he cannot find. Willy thought that the trouble was that he was getting too old to sell, that he needed more dynamism, or drive, or creativity, psychological traits to buoy up a psychological being in a universe of tensions and suspension. His universe was more complex than Oedipus's and really it was more ghastly than Oedipus's, too. Willy was left with a kind of nothingness; he was a nobody, his atoms were ready for the ash-can. For him there is no sin, no retribution, no Grace, and ultimately, no peace.

This then is how it stacks up. Jocasta finds out that she is wife to her son and she puts her head in a noose. Oedipus finds out that he is husband to his mother and pierces his eyes so that he will not have to look at himself or at his children-brothers. Linda finds out nothing and goes on living meaninglessly. Willy, still blind, attempts to die grandly like a Sophoclean king, and he kills himself by ramming his car. That is about as everyday a death as you can find.

Death of a Salesman and *Oedipus Rex*—both present grim, soul-searching, moving business. The question of all the ages echoes in both: "Who am I?" Now I know why Willy Loman was in that bookshop window in the Netherlands. This is the question of everyman of every place of every time, relevant eternally—asked or unasked.

Death of a Salesman, then, is more than an American drama about a salesman. It is that to be sure. But basically all human beings are salesmen; all wear the salesman's mask. This play reveals more than the weakness of Willy's dream, more than the weakness of the American dream: it reveals the basic problem of self-knowledge that each human being must face. In this sense Arthur Miller shows us the form and pressure of our time. He cries out with the Delphic Oracle, "Know Thyself." And it is this phrase that we find inscribed on Oedipus's tomb and on Willy's simple grave.

Willy Loman and King Lear

Paul N. Siegel

About two hundred years ago George Lillo, declaring that tragedy need not concern itself solely with kings, wrote *The London Merchant.* Highly popular in his day and for a long time after that, it is now, with its cheap sentimentality and naive moralizing, taken seriously by no one as tragedy or, for that matter, as drama of any kind. In our own time Arthur Miller too has sought in the widely acclaimed *Death of a Salesman,* as he indicated in an essay in *The New York Times* (27 February 1949), to write a tragedy of the common man. Will *Death of a Salesman* meet the same fate as its predecessor?

It is my opinion that Miller's play is a successful tragedy and that, because it is, a comparison between the drama of Willy Loman and his sons and *King Lear,* Shakespeare's drama of a father and his daughters, will reveal several interesting fundamental similarities. In making this comparison, I am not, of course, suggesting that it is of the same order of merit as the world's greatest tragedy but that it is a viable representative of the same rare species.

Both plays may be said to have as their themes the philosophical dictum "Know thyself." The cause of the catastrophe of the king of ancient Briton and that of the salesman of today is the same: each does not know himself and the world in which he is living. Lear has, as Regan says, "ever but slenderly known himself." He has been so impressed by the pomp and power of his position as king that he has lost any sense of human limitations. This he recovers only after he has been exposed to the storm: "They told me I was every thing; 'tis a lie, I am not ague-proof." In casting off Cordelia for her statement that she loves him as nature demands her to love him, that she cannot give all her love to him and none to her

Paul Siegel, "Willy Loman and King Lear," *College English* 17 (March 1956), 341–345. Reprinted by permission of the publisher.

husband, he is disregarding the law of nature, which governs all, kings as well as commoners.

So too Willy Loman is, as Biff says at the end, a man "who never knew who he was." He does not know his relation to his world, which is governed by no eternal law of nature but by social laws rising from the nature of a particular civilization. In disregarding social reality he ruins his sons by holding out before them his vision of triumph. Willy lives by the gospel that if one "sells one's self" he can rise to great heights. However, as we see in the scene with Howard, personality actually does not count in the impersonal world of business. Howard, absorbed in the wire recorder, which he says is "the most terrific machine I ever saw in my life," pays no attention to Willy and his talk of service to the firm. In this world, in which machines rather than human beings are important and individuals are only so many counters in the game of business, Willy thinks that he and his sons will reach the top because they are well liked.

What shatters his life and Biff's is not merely an accidental discovery of a casual deception. It is the revelation of the falsehood that is Willy's existence. Lonely and insecure in his world of impersonal relationships governed by the market, Willy must deceive himself if he is to live by his gospel of popularity. He boasts, "Be liked and you will never want. You take me, for instance. I never have to wait in line to see a buyer," but he finds it necessary to use the woman in Boston not only as a means to deaden his aching sense of loneliness but as a means by which he can get through to the buyers before the other salesmen.

In Willy's floundering self-contradictions there is a grim, ironic humor, something of the kind present in the Fool's repeated sallies about the topsy-turvy absurdity of Lear's having given the authority of the kingship to his daughters. Willy's folly is shown to be as absurd as Lear's, as, through the reversions to the past of his distraught mind, he brings before us the sardonic contrast between his dream of what Biff was to be and what he has become. Reliving the past and yet not recognizing his criminal miseducation of his sons, he winks at Young Biff's practicing with a football he has stolen from the school, saying that the coach would probably congratulate him on his initiative if he knew, and then wonders, "Why is he stealing? What did I tell him? I never in my life told him anything but decent things." Just as he wavers between the desire to have his sons cultivate the virtues of rugged individualism (the stock exchange is full of "fearless characters," Ben assures him) and an uneasy regard for the rules of prudential middleclass morality, so he wavers between the conflicting maxims of salesmanship. "Walk in very serious," he tells Biff with one breath, advising him concerning an interview that is crucial only in his imagination, and adds in the next breath, "Walk in with a big laugh." "Start big and you'll end big . . . And if anything falls off the desk . . . don't you pick it up," he counsels—and he himself, when he sees Howard, hands him the cigarette lighter from his desk and pleads for just a small salary, continuing to lower the amount he will accept. We are reminded of the cruel humor of the proud Lear's self-abasement in going from daughter to daughter, as each reduces the number of knights he may have.

This grim humor only heightens the pathos of Willy Loman's predicament, as, lost and bewildered as a rat scurrying about in a maze, he desperately searches for his lost dream. "The way they boxed us in here," he exclaims. So too Lear, towering figure though he be, is seen at times as "a poor, infirm, weak, and despised old man" whose piteous torment reminds us of Gloucester's words, "As flies to wanton boys are we to the gods,/ They kill us for their sport."

But, of course, Gloucester's words do not represent the final impression of the play. The suffering of the good is seen to be not cruelly indifferent mockery by the governing powers of the universe but a divinely conferred blessing which purges them of their selfishness: the dignity of man is re-affirmed. In *Death of a Salesman* this sense of human dignity conquers our impression of Willy as a rat in a maze. Our civilization, unlike the divine government of the universe in *King Lear,* is not exonerated, but humanity protests against it. "You can't eat the orange and throw the peel away—a man is not a piece of fruit," Willy tells Howard. Although Willy is boxed in and baffled by his society, the insistence on his dignity as a human being, voiced by Linda as well as himself, together with the implication that, difficult though it might have been, he could have freed himself of his dream, prevents us from seeing him as small and insignificant. Moreover, if he has been fatally unable to distinguish between dream and reality, the intensity of his attempt to realize it and his readiness to sacrifice everything for his sons evokes admiration. Typical and ordinary as he is, he has something of the greatness of spirit of King Lear. When, picking his way blindly to the restaurant washroom, toward which he has been led by Biff and where he is to be found by the waiter on his knees pounding the floor, he is reduced to his lowest depths of dignity, Biff reminds us of the true nobility that was his: "Miss Forsythe, you've just seen a prince walk by. A fine, troubled prince. A hard-working, unappreciated prince." Just so when Lear, fantastically dressed with wild flowers, ludicrously dashes off, uttering a hunter's cry as if to urge on to their game the attendants he believes have been sent by his daughters to apprehend him, the gentleman recalls the greatness from which this is such a decline: "A sight most pitiful in the meanest wretch,/ Past speaking of in a king!"

What happens to Willy Loman, like what happens to King Lear, elicits not merely pity but fear. In *Lear* this comes from the seeming shaking of what the audience has been taught to regard as the eternal verities, as the wicked prosper and universal chaos appears to be impending. In *Death of a Salesman* it comes from the audience's realization that Willy's dream, the great American dream which it has been taught to accept, has misled and destroyed him. It is this perception, fully conscious or not, which theatre spectators experience. They are not just feeling sorry for a pathetic person; in a profound sense each of them feels that he *is* Willy Loman.

For the Elizabethan audience a king, while greater than other men, was not of a different order of being. He was a magnification of ordinary humanity, with superior powers of reason but a correspondingly greater intensity of emotion which could destroy him as passion could destroy every man. While the audience regarded the tragic hero with respectful awe, it was thus also able to identify itself with him, to feel that "the death of Antony/ Is not a single doom; in the name lay/ A moiety of the world." The tragedy of the king was the tragedy of his people; his frailties were not his alone but the frailties of mankind; his suffering and death were the expiation every man has to make for his sins, and they were also—as in the crucifixion of Christ and the expulsion of the regal scapegoat in the agricultural folk ceremonies of Elizabethan England—an expiation *for* every man, the conclusion of his tragedy bringing the restoration of social order. Lear, stripped of his attendants, made a mock-king, and driven out into the storm, acts as such a scapegoat.

So too Willy Loman the salesman acts as an image of ourselves. For, as Erich Fromm has observed in *Escape from Freedom* (pp.

119–120), we are all of us, in the modern world, concerned, like Willy, with "selling" ourselves, the members of the middle class in a particular sense:

> The businessman, the physician, the clerical employee, sell their "personality." They have to have a "personality" if they are to sell their products or services. . . . If there is no use for the qualities a person offers, he *has* none; just as an unsalable commodity is valueless though it might have its use value. Thus, the self-confidence, the "feeling of self," is merely an indication of what others think of the person. It is not he who is convinced of his value regardless of popularity and his success on the market. If he is sought after, he is somebody; if he is not popular, he is simply nobody.

Willy is thus the apotheosis of the common man. He sacrifices himself so that his son Biff may realize himself, may cash in on his personality: "Can you imagine that magnificence with twenty thousand dollars in his pocket?"

And in a sense his sacrifice is not in vain; in a sense the seed which he plants in his garden as he plans his suicide comes to fruition. For Biff has learned who he is as a result of seeing his father's crowning degradation while acknowledging his love for his father and coming to respect him. Biff has been educated by experience, as Albany has learned the nature of evil and Edgar has learned wisdom through adversity. Biff's finding himself at the end contributes to a sense of reconciliation, as does the restoration of order with the assumption of the kingship by Albany, with Edgar as his counselor. So too does the feeling that Willy, like Lear, is freed by death from the "rack of this tough world" contribute to this sense of reconciliation. "I made the last payment on the house today," says Linda over Willy's body. "Today, dear. And there'll be nobody home. We're free and clear." As she says these words, sobs rise from her throat, the suffocating grief that made her beg "Help me, Willy, I can't cry" is released, and she repeats, "We're free. . . . We're free. . . . We're free. . . ." There is, of course, dramatic irony in Willy's dying just when his house is finally his, but there is also in her concluding words a feeling of release from the tyrannical dream of Willy. Finally, Charley's elegiac summation of Willy's life, like Albany's concluding couplet referring to Lear's strength and endurance, further helps to reconcile us to his death: "Nobody dast blame this man. You don't understand: Willy was a salesman. And for a salesman, there is no rock bottom to the life. . . . A salesman is got to dream, boy. It comes with the territory." Even Willy's dream of his magnificent funeral turns out wrong, with only Charley and Willy's family attending. But Charley's words remind us that, tragically mistaken though Willy was, his capacity to dream and to struggle commands respect.

Death of a Salesman:
An Appreciation

Lois Gordon

Willy Loman, the salesman who sacrifices himself upon the altar of the American dream, has become as much of an American culture hero as Huck Finn. Like Twain's boy, Willy has met with enormous public success and is capable of moving the middle-brow audience as well as the intellectual sophisticate. The latter, however, has belabored *Death of a Salesman* to no end with two questions: Is the play primarily a socio-political criticism of American culture, or, does Willy Loman fall far enough to be a tragic figure?

While these issues are continually provocative, they, as Miller points out in his famous Introduction to the *Collected Plays,* have been explored ad nauseum and to the point of meaninglessness. Perhaps Miller's stand arises from his awareness that either conclusion is too simple and too pat, each utterly destroying the other's possibility. Certainly a play cannot be both tragic and social, as Eric Bentley notes, for the two forms conflict in purpose. Social drama treats the little man as victim and arouses pity but no terror (for man is too little and passive to be the tragic figure), whereas tragedy destroys the possibility of social drama, since the tragic catharsis "reconciles us to, or persuades us to disregard precisely those material conditions which the social drama calls our attention to and protests against."

It seems to me that the brilliance of *Death of a Salesman* lies precisely in its reconciliation of these apparent contrarieties, that Arthur Miller has created a sort of narrative poem whose overall purpose can be understood only by a consideration of its poetic as

Lois Gordon, "*Death of a Salesman*: An Appreciation," in *The Forties: Fiction, Poetry, Drama,* ed. Warren French (Deland, Florida: Everett/Edwards, 1969), pp. 273–83. Reprinted by permission of the publisher.

well as narrative elements. *Death of a Salesman*, the major American drama of the 1940s, remains unequalled in its brilliant and original fusion of realistic and poetic techniques, its richness of visual and verbal texture, and its wide range of emotional impact.

The drama of the 30s (including Miller's first plays at the University of Michigan and even his later *All My Sons*) leaned too heavily upon the depiction of social forces that were not emotionally recognizable. The emotional, or if you will, the poetic realization of man's totality was lost in the oversimplification of conflicting social and moral ideologies. The plays were external and linear; they moved to a single climax. The central issue of *All My Sons,* for example—man's responsibility to his society—was just too clearcut, and its protagonist's realization of this had too much of a lightningbolt quality. Although its social issues were meaningful and competently portrayed, Miller gained no sense of inner reality, of his hero's emotional struggle for truth, self-realization and self-understanding.

The drama of the 50s and 60s, generally speaking, lies at the other end of the spectrum, for this theater relies upon emotion without perceivable social or psychological context. The term "total theater," Artaud's original concept of a theater that would hit to the heart of its audience's emotion, has been very popular as a theory since the early 50s. Nevertheless, most of its embodiments have been in mad, free form, or perhaps formless, orgiastic rituals, where audience and actor rollick together somewhere across the footlights. Those who feel that there is a point beyond which form cannot bend without breaking and the art object ceasing to exist, while applauding the "experimental," find the emotion of revulsion more powerful than those presumably being communicated. But these plays are said to reflect the times, the anguish of an age where meaning has been destroyed, personality fragmented, and man alienated from man. The use of visual poetry, the stage as metaphor, existential anguish as a central theme, fragmentation of logic in time and space—all these are said to help us in evolving a new awareness of ourselves. But somewhere, when we watch all this, although we may be moved, we have the feeling that life, in the terms that we know it, of the daily questions of how to get along with one's father or sons or boss, or how to find, in rather ordinary terms, an ideal by which to live, are lost. The events that go on stage—really poetic attempts to involve us emotionally—are, in a sense, too abstract. We want meaning in a play or any literary form, but we also want to recognize our own lives.

Miller succeeds, where so many of his 30s and 60s contemporaries fail, in fusing all of these disparate elements. He presents a sort of total theater and, in a sense, is the transitional genius of the American stage, 1930–69. As Eliot might say, on the one hand he represents the turning point of the literary current, for he continues the human values and forms of the past in the terms of the present. He concentrates upon human endeavor and heroism with the contemporary fragmented, anguished (in existential terms) world of the middle class citizen. But on the other hand, considering once again the drama preceding and following *Death of a Salesman,* he recreates a total theater by harmonizing subjective and objective realism, or in theatrical jargon, expressionism and realism.

As Miller notes in his Introductory essay, the fundamental problem in a play is to create within the framework of a realistic statement symbolic significance which arises organically from that realistic frame. The central issue, it would seem, is action as metaphor. The meaning of life, or an understanding of life, as seen in a protagonist's commitment to social, psychological, and metaphysical (tragic) issues, must be inherent in the dramatic situation. Intellectual understanding, or meaning in a discursive sense, must be, much as Eliot has noted, wedded to emotional perception.

In a sense, to consider whether Miller's work is solely social or tragic is to split this unified sensibility. It is to deny that Miller's drama builds upon, to borrow another of Eliot's phrases, the objective correlative to gain its richness and complexity of texture. One recalls Eliot's famous dictum:

> The only way of expressing emotion in the form of art is by finding an "objective correlative"; in other words, a set of objects, a situation, a chain of events which shall be the formula of that *particular* emotion, such that when the external facts, which must terminate in sensory experience, are given, the emotion is immediately evoked.[1]

That Miller's concern is with this sort of total effect is apparent in his comment:

[1]Thomas Stearns Eliot, "Hamlet and His Problems," *The Sacred Wand*, 3rd ed. (London: Methuen, 1932), p. 100.

The metaphor is everything, the symbolized action, the action which is much greater than itself and is yet concrete is what we're after, I think. I think the structure of a play should be its essential poem—what it leaves out. And what it follows to a real climax. Before there can be the other poetry, there must be that.

Death of a Salesman succeeds by Eliot's and Miller's standards. Miller finds the appropriate concrete symbols for the social realities of his time and place. He achieves through a series of emotional confrontations among the members of a single family an emotionally valid psychological statement about the particular conflicts of the American family, as well as the universal psychological family struggle. And by placing all of these events within the context of one man's thoughts, rambling over his past and present life, he achieves an internal drama of a man's epic journey to self-knowledge through experience. The entire play is, in this last sense, a recognition scene.

On the social level, Willy is a victim of the American dream, personified in all its confusion by three different figures. First, there is Ben, Willy's brother, the self-made man who went into the (capitalist) jungle and came out rich, the totally self-assured man who knew what he wanted and would brook no ethical interference with his designs for material success. "Never fight fair with a stranger" is Ben's motto. For him, ruggedness, rather than personality or personal integrity, is the key to success: "Who ever liked J.P. Morgan?"

But the dream is also symbolized by Dave Singleman, the salesman who lived on trains and in strange cities, and who, by virtue of some incandescent, irresistible personal loveableness, built his frame and fortune. Finally, the dream is symbolized, in perhaps its most noble embodiment, by Willy's father, who not only ventured into a pioneer's wilderness with no security or assurance of success, but who was also a creator, a man whose avocation was as well his vocation, a man who made flutes and high music.

Willy, as victim of this inexorable social system which drives its men to frantic, all-consuming dreams of success, is doomed not only by their grandiosity but also by their inherent contradictoriness. And as social victim, he is given his elegy in the last scene by his friend Charley, who, ironically, by a kind of indifference and lack of dream, has succeeded within the American system. Charley points out that a salesman must dream of great things if he is to travel the territory "way out there in the blue," but that he is also a man who really has no trade like the carpenter, lawyer, or doctor, and when the brilliant smile that has brought his success begins to pale, he must fall, though "there is no rock bottom."

Because this portrait rings true, the play seems to indict a system that promises and indeed demands total commitment to success without regard to human values, a system that, as Willy says to Howard, will "eat the orange and throw the peel away." Miller, in this sense, does attack the society that says "business is business," where the cruel inhuman son can replace his kindly father and say to a longtime employee, who gave him his Christian name, "Look, kid, I'm busy this morning."

It is a system symbolized ultimately in the play by the car, that strange, uniquely American obsession, which Willy and his sons (in Willy's glorious recollection in the first act) polish, love and cherish as a manifestation of their manly glory. But the car is something that wears out and breaks down, and soon enough, unless one can afford an ever-shinier, newer one, he is driving an old Studebaker, smashed up many times, with a broken carburetor. He is driving the symbol of an outlived usefulness.

The road is also part of this symbol. The road his father travelled in a covered wagon, by sheer ruggedness, individuality and courage, becomes early in Willy's lifetime the road to territories not ever opened, but it ultimately becomes the hellish road beside which the woods burn, and it no longer leads anywhere. In the end, the road, which had idealistic as well as realistic meaning for his father, is merely a journey devoid of significance. Meaning in Willy's life lies in the scenery beside the road—in the beautiful elms and the hills, in the creative sense of a spiritualized nature.

If it appears that Willy's dilemma is purely social, Miller cautions against this final interpretation. Charley, he reminds us, is Willy's counterbalance, and he is a man of humanity. His loyalty to Willy has a sincere, saintly quality. Though he gets furious at Willy, calls him stupid, proud, and childish, he remains faithful to a man for whom he has affection. Despite his material success, which undoubtedly pleases him, he has never been corrupted by the myth of success, nor has he ever lost the sense of human relatedness.

Even more than this social theme, it is undeniably Miller's psychological drama—his story of a family with its multiple loves and antagonisms, its conflicting aims and yet total involvement—

that drives his audience to tears shortly after the play's beginning. Miller's psychological setting is particularly America, for we are largely a second and third generation country.

The first generation (Willy's father) has been forced, in order to make a living, to break up the family. But, while Willy's father achieved and was creative, he left behind him a wife, a young son-become-fatherless, and an older son driven to find success at the expense of love.

Willy, the second generation, is his father's victim. While he wants to love and "do right" by his sons—his poignant "Was I right?" echoes throughout his lifetime—he is driven to use them as heirs to the kingdom that he believes must be built. Thus, he must pass on to them not only love but the doomed dream. He cannot relent even now, in the present time of play, with his son thirty-four years old, a boy obviously not destined to achieve the greatness Willy wanted for him. Willy must still, at the expense of endless quarrels and his son's hatred and contempt, give Biff minute instructions in big business morality: "Tell him you were in the business in the West. Not farm work." "And if anything falls off the desk . . . don't you pick it up. They have office boys for that." "And don't undersell yourself. No less than fifteen thousand dollars." Willy must perpetuate that now hollow ideal that is his father's legacy.

Yet because Willy did remain at home with his mother and receive more in the way of love and human affection, he has come to know their value. For this reason he stays in New York with his wife Linda, whom he loves, rather than go to the New Continent; he looks forward to being with his boys more than travelling, and, at the play's end, he finally knows an exultant peace in a momentary spiritual communion with his son.

In recalling his father, Willy says to Ben in pride: "Please tell about Dad. I want my boys to hear. I want them to know the kind of stock they spring from." But his comment is filled with an anguish that permeates and gives richness to Willy as a man: "Dad left when I was such a baby and I never had a chance to talk to him and I still feel—kind of temporary about myself." Willy has searched for a father's approval throughout his life, through living out his fantasy of what his father was and would have wanted. So too, Willy's sons are trapped by their father's fantasy, even more hollow for them, and its fulfillment remains their means to gain his love.

A revealing example of this is both Biff's thievery and Willy's approval, virtually a logical extension of the same "You can get away with it" fantasy that is Willy's: if you are beautiful enough, you can steal and the coach will approve. Biff, even before his disillusionment in the final scene, chronologically in his life at age seventeen, has been destroyed by his acceptance of Willy's dream. Biff has always felt that to gain his father's love, he had to be The Best—the most beautiful and most popular boy, the football hero and All-American. Yet somewhere he has known that his father loved him and that this love did not solely depend on appearance. All the same, because so much of their relationship has hinged on Biff's being special, a kind of "Adonis" in Willy's eyes, so too Willy has had to be godlike in Biff's eyes. Rather than enjoying and appreciating the emotion they share, they have had to relate through the medium of their common fantasy. But with the episode in Boston, Biff's immaculate father fantasy has broken once and for all time, and Biff has spent the next seventeen years of his life living in a twilight world somewhere between the sunshine and trees, the free life that his father also loves which, as Biff says at the end of the play, "was the best part of him," and the nightmare of stockrooms, empty roads, continual smiles, and phony charm that he has absorbed from his father as necessary to both success and parental love.

Biff is the third generation, a representative of the sons of the middle class for whom the middle class dream has failed but for whom the only alternatives are various, all-embracing idealisms totally free from social structure. He is the beatnik, the hippie, and the radical, in whom one cannot help but see that the potent part of idealism is rebellion against the father and the father's way of life but in whom a desperate longing for father-love remains.

Hap, the younger son, less favored by nature and his father, perhaps as Willy was in comparison with Ben, has escaped the closeness with his father that destroys Biff in social terms. Thus worshipping his father from afar, Hap has never fully come to realize that phony part of his father and his father's dreams. He does have longings to be outdoors and to get away from the crippling fifty-weeks-of-work-a-year routine, but because he has never seen his father's feet of clay, he has more fully than Biff accepted his father's dream. He is not a social rebel, and he will carry on with the life of a salesman, and, one suspects, go on to the death of a salesman. He will violate the boss' wife out of some lonely desperation, as Willy sought support and solace in his Boston woman. He will also prove his manliness with fast cars and fancy talk, but again like Willy, he will never really believe in his own manliness in any mature way. Just as Willy is called a kid throughout, and referred to as the diminutive Willy by everyone except Ben, ("Willy, when are you going to grow up?" asks Charley more than once), Happy has been trapped by the infantile American *Playboy* magazine vision of the male.

Linda, as the eternal wife and mother, the fixed point of affection both given and received, the woman who suffers and endures is, in many ways, the earth mother who embodies the play's ultimate moral value—love. But in the beautiful, ironic complexity of her creation, she is also Willy's and their sons' destroyer. In her love Linda has accepted Willy's greatness and his dream, but while in her admiration for Willy her love is powerful and moving, in her admiration for his dreams, it is lethal. She encourages Willy's dream, yet she will not let him leave her for the New Continent, the only realm where the dream can be fulfilled. She wants to reconcile father and son, but she attempts this in the context of Willy's false values: She cannot allow her sons to achieve that selfhood that involves denial of these values.

While these are the basic social and psychological themes of the play, they subserve its central theme.

Miller notes in his comments on *Death of a Salesman* that he initially intended to write a monodrama—a play called *The Inside of His Head*—which would re-create a man's entire life in terms of past and present, by means of his recollections at a particular point of self-reevaluation late in life. This is really the play Miller has written. *Death of a Salesman* is a drama of a man's journey into himself; it is a man's emotional recapitulation of the experiences that have shaped him and his values, a man's confession of the dreams to which he has been committed; and it is also a man's attempt to confront, in what is ultimately a metaphysical sense, the meaning of his life and the nature of his universe.

The play has been criticized because there is no recognition scene in the traditional sense. There is a notable absence, it has been said, of the classic, tragic, articulated awareness of self-delusion and final understanding. But, in emotional terms, the entire play is really a long recognition scene. Willy's heroism and stature derive not from an intellectual grandeur but from the fact that, in an emotional way, he confronts himself and his world. As

Lear in madness comes to truth, so does Willy Loman. Miller has pointed out that social laws have replaced fate as man's inexorable enemy, and we might add as their helpmate, psychological determinism.

The play begins at what is basically that moment of anguish that Camus has talked of in *The Myth of Sisyphus,* that moment when the order of things, fragments, where the ordinary social realities and values, in Willy's case the American success dream, are no longer adequate. The road and Willy's car, for all their social and psychological significance, have metaphysical meaning. Willy's soul can no longer travel the road; it has broken down because the road has lost meaning. That multiplicity within himself, his creative yearnings, and that part of himself which sees creativity as a moral value, now intrudes on consciousness. The woods burn, and he is thrown into a hell of disorder and conflicting value within himself. The two bags which are his salesgoods, his emblems of material success, the two bags which his sons would carry into the capitals of New England and so carry on the tradition of his dream, are now too heavy. His sons will never bear them for him, and the values which they represent are now the overwhelming burden of his existence.

The refrigerator and the house, though paid for, will never house the totality of his yearnings. They will never be the monuments to his existence that he has sought to make them. His sons, who would also have been the immortality of his dreams, his mark on the world, have failed him. As the play progresses and Willy's sons finally leave him kneeling in a bathroom to take their chippies, in consonance with the manliness they have learned from him, they leave him alone to face the void within his soul.

In the play Willy has no traditional religion; his religion has been the American Dream; his gods have been Dave Singleman, Ben, and his father, but they are now all dead—to the world and as meaningful values for himself. When Willy goes to Howard to demand his just due and winds up confronting a babbling recording machine, which he cannot turn off, he is confronting the impersonal technologic society which metes out its own impersonal justice. But he is also confronting a world without justice, a world where final truth is a babble. Ironically, the capitals which elsewhere function as symbols of the pioneer spirit and Willy's pride in his own travels, are now controlled by a child, and Willy's own sword of battle is turned against him.

The play is about *the death* of a salesman. The wares which Willy has sold, as well as being symbolic of his role in a capitalistic society, are, as Miller has said, "himself." In the final analysis, it does not matter what he sold, or in objective terms, how well he succeeded.

The particulars concerning Willy's situation also have universal significance. Willy has lived passionately for values to which he is committed, and he comes to find that they are false and inadequate. He has loved his sons with a passion which wanted for them that which would destroy them. He has grown old and he will soon vanish without a trace, and he discovers really the vanity of all human endeavor, save perhaps love. His foolishness is really no greater than Othello's raving jealousy or Lear's appreciation of the insincere, outward appearance of love. A pension would not help him, nor, had he come to be J.P. Morgan would it have helped. Linda says, "A small man can be just as exhausted as a great man," and she cries out "Attention must be paid." Inevitably, no matter what material heights a man succeeds to, his life is brief and his comprehension finite, while the universe remains infinite and incomprehensible. Willy comes to face, if you will, the absurdity of life, and it is for this reason that attention must be paid.

The vehicle for his realization is the play, which is the poem of his life. As in a poem, intensity is built through images of multiple meaning, through rhythmic repetition, through a logic of association, through an evocation of emotional intensities, through a time sequence which is subjective, and, appropriate for a poem of the theater, through visual and auditory imagery and leit-motifs handled as metaphors.

The flute music is his father's flute, the music of his father's life and the music of Willy's dream. The entire stage setting is transparent with objective and subjective experience occupying the same space, much as if they are equivalent to and intermingle inextricably in a man's life. Lighting is used to echo Willy's emotional states. Images—car, road, refrigerator, valises, silk stockings, a woman's laughter—through their rhythmic reappearance in the past and present, in different contexts, grow into symbols of his entire life. This is the poetry of the play. That the language itself is not traditionally poetic is only to say that it is no less so than Yeats' description of his heart as a rag and bone shop,the form no more traditionally poetic than the fragments of *The Waste Land*. The imagery is drawn from the hard cold facts of the life of a particular man—Willy Loman, the salesman for the Wagner Company, who lives in a house in Brooklyn. It grows in meaning by association and juxtaposition to metaphysical significance. Willy's death is not just his driving a car to a suicide which will bring some much needed money to his family. It is Willy's soul in triumphant revenge upon the dream that has broken him. It is a final act of will in defiance of a chaos which he cannot end, it is made possible by the realization of a human value, his son's love, which he cannot live by, because the world is too complex, but which he can die for. If it is ironic, it is because fate, social law, psychological law, and the illusions of life are necessary, inevitable and always, of course, victorious over the individual man in the end.

Chronology

	Miller	*The Age*
1915	Born in Manhattan, New York City, 17 October, second son of Isadore and Augusta Miller	
1916		Sinking of Lusitania; United States enters World War I
1918		Armistice ends World War I
1929	Family moves to Brooklyn	Stock market crash, 24 October
1930		Sinclair Lewis first American to win Nobel Prize for Literature
1932	Graduates from Abraham Lincoln High School; goes to work in an automobile parts warehouse	Franklin D. Roosevelt elected the 32nd President of the United States
1933		Adolf Hitler becomes Chancellor of Germany
1934	Enters University of Michigan at Ann Arbor	
1936	*Honors at Dawn* wins Avery Hopwood Award ($250) and production at university	Hitler invades Rhineland, 17 March; Civil War breaks out in Spain, 17 July
1938	*No Villain* (later retitled *They Too Arise*) wins Avery Hopwood Award and production at university and the Theatre Guild Bureau of New Plays prize	
1938	B.A. University of Michigan Goes to work for Federal Theatre Project	Hitler invades Austria, 10 April; Munich Pact gives Germany the Sudetenland, 29 September

	Miller	*The Age*
1939		Hitler invades Poland, beginning World War II
1940	Marries Mary Grace Slattery	Hemingway's *For Whom the Bell Tolls* is published.
1941		Japanese bomb Pearl Harbor, 7 December; United States enters World War II
1944	Tours army camps gathering material for film, *The Story of GI Joe*; prose account, *Situation Normal,* published; *The Man Who Had All the Luck* produced in New York	Roosevelt elected for fourth term
1945	*Focus,* a novel, published	Roosevelt dies, 12 April; victory in Europe, 7 May; atomic bomb dropped, 9 August; victory over Japan, 14 August
1946		First meeting, United Nations General Assembly, 10 January
1947	*All My Sons* produced in New York	
1948		UN creates state of Israel; Truman defeats Dewey for presidency
1949	*Death of a Salesman* produced in New York	
1950	*An Enemy of the People,* adapted from Ibsen, produced in New York	"McCarthy Era" begins attacks on suspected communists
1953	*The Crucible* produced in New York	Eisenhower becomes 34th President
1954	Refused passport for opening of *The Crucible* in Brussels	Army-McCarthy hearings
1955	*A Memory of Two Mondays* and *A View from the Bridge* produced together in New York	

	Miller	*The Age*
1956	Divorced from Mary Slattery; married to Marilyn Monroe, 29 June	
1957	*Collected Plays* published; convicted of contempt of Congress for refusing to name suspected communists	Federal legislation to integrate schools in United States
1958	Conviction unanimously reversed by United States Supreme Court	Russia launches Sputnik
1960	Filming of *The Misfits*; separated from Marilyn Monroe	John F. Kennedy becomes 35th President; Fidel Castro takes over Cuba
1961	Divorced from Marilyn Monroe, 20 January	
1962	Marries Ingeborg Morath; Marilyn Monroe dies	Cuban missile crisis
1963	*Jane's Blanket* published (children's story)	Assassination of President Kennedy, 22 November
1964	*After the Fall* and *Incident at Vichy* produced separately in New York	
1965		U.S. combat forces in Viet Nam
1967	*I Don't Need You Any More*	"Six-Day War" between Arabs and Israelis
1968	*The Price* produced in New York	Robert Kennedy assassinated, 5 June
1969		U.S. lands a man on the moon, 20 June
1970	*Fame* produced in New York	
1971		Pentagon papers published; China admitted to United Nations
1972	*The Creation of the World and Other Business*	Richard Nixon elected for second term as 37th President

	Miller	*The Age*
1973		Cease-fire in Viet Nam, 27 January
1974	*Up from Paradise* produced at Ann Arbor	Watergate scandal forces the resignation of Richard Nixon
1976		U. S. Bicentennial
1977	*The Archbishop's Ceiling* produced in Washington; *In the Country* (with Ingeborg Morath) and *The Theatre Essays of Arthur Miller* published	
1978	Visits China with his wife	
1979	*American Clock* and *Chinese Encounters* published	
1980		U.S. boycotts Olympic Games because Russia occupies Afghanistan
1981	*Playing for Time,* television adaptation of Fanya Fenelon's book, wins an Emmy	

Notes on Contributors

HELENE KOON is Professor of English at California State College, San Bernardino. She has published articles and books on eighteenth-century drama and is co-author (with Richard Switzer) of *Eugene Scribe,* a biography of the playwright.

BARCLAY W. BATES was teaching English at Lowell High School in San Francisco, California, when this article was written.

BRADFORD S. FIELD, JR., is Professor of English at Wayne State University. His most recent work is *Shakespeare's Julius Caesar: A Production Collection.* Chicago: Nelson-Hall, 1980.

LOIS GORDON is Professor of English at Fairleigh Dickinson University. Her specialty is twentieth-century American drama, and she has written articles on Randall Jarrell, James Purdy, and Richard Eberhardt.

SIGHLE A. KENNEDY is Associate Professor of English at Hunter College. She has written articles on Yeats, Samuel Beckett, and James Joyce.

STEPHEN LAWRENCE was teaching English at Carnegie Institute of Technology when this article was written.

ARTHUR K. OBERG is Professor of English at the University of Washington, Seattle. He has written on Samuel Beckett and Marcel Proust. His most recent work is *Modern American Lyric: Lowell, Berryman, Creely and Plath.* New Brunswick, N.J.: Rutgers University Press, 1978.

CHARLOTTE F. OTTEN is Associate Professor of English at Calvin College, Michigan. She has written articles on Donne, Milton, and contemporary literature.

BRIAN PARKER is Professor of English at Trinity College, University of Toronto. His specialty is American literature and drama.

PAUL N. SIEGEL is Professor of English at Long Island University. He is the author of many journal articles on Shakespeare, and his most recent work is *Revolution of the Twentieth-Century Novel*. New York: Monad Press, 1979.

DENNIS WELLAND is Professor of American literature at the University of Manchester, England. He edited the *Journal of American Studies* for ten years and has published many books and articles on drama.

Selected Bibliography

FERGUSON, ALFRED R. "The Tragedy of the American Dream in *Death of a Salesman*," *Thought*, 53 (March 1978), 83–98.

GELB, PHILIP. "A Matter of Happiness in *Death of a Salesman*," in *Two Modern Tragedies*, ed. John Hurrell. New York: Scribner's, 1961, pp. 76–88.

HAGOPIAN, JOHN V. "Arthur Miller: The Salesman's Two Cases," *Modern Drama*, 6 (1963–64), 117–125.

HARSHBARGER, KARL. *The Burning Jungle: An Analysis of Arthur Miller's Death of a Salesman.* Boston: University Press of America, 1980.

HOGAN, ROBERT. *Arthur Miller.* Pamphlets on American Writers, no. 40. Minneapolis: University of Minnesota Press, 1964.

HUFTEL, SHEILA. *Arthur Miller: The Burning Glass.* New York: Citadel, 1965.

MCMAHON, HELEN M. "Arthur Miller's Common Man: The Problem of Realistic and Mythic," *Drama and Theatre*, 10 (1972), 128–33.

NELSON, BENJAMIN. *Arthur Miller: Portrait of a Playwright.* New York: McKay, 1967.

TROWBRIDGE, CLINTON. "Arthur Miller: Between Pathos and Tragedy," *Modern Drama*, 10 (1967), 221–32.

WEALES, GERALD. *Death of a Salesman: Text and Criticism.* New York: Viking, 1967.

WILLIAMS, RAYMOND. "The Realism of Arthur Miller," *Critical Quarterly*, 1 (1959), 140–49.